The MANHATTAN PROJECT TRINITY TEST

The
MANHATTAN PROJECT TRINITY TEST

Witnessing the Bomb in New Mexico

Elva K. Österreich

Published by The History Press
Charleston, SC
www.historypress.com

Back cover: The only color photo taken of the Trinity Test. It was taken by photographer Jack Aeby. This photo is usually seen in reverse, but that is incorrect. This is the actual view the camera would have taken as the atomic age began in the early morning of July 16, 1945. *Public domain.*

First published 2020

Manufactured in the United States

ISBN 9781467144421

Library of Congress Control Number: 2020941860

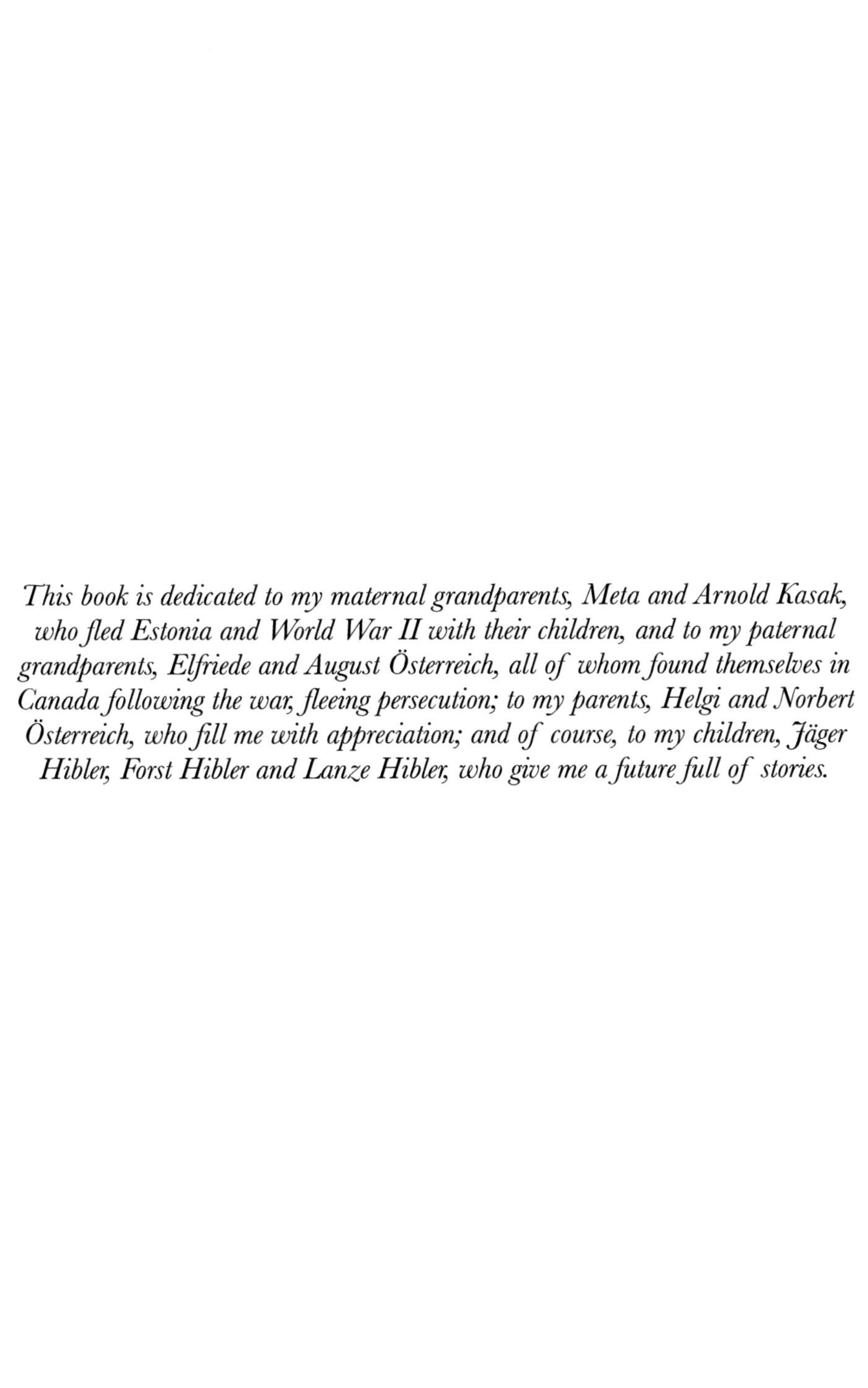

This book is dedicated to my maternal grandparents, Meta and Arnold Kasak, who fled Estonia and World War II with their children, and to my paternal grandparents, Elfriede and August Österreich, all of whom found themselves in Canada following the war, fleeing persecution; to my parents, Helgi and Norbert Österreich, who fill me with appreciation; and of course, to my children, Jäger Hibler, Forst Hibler and Lanze Hibler, who give me a future full of stories.

CONTENTS

ACKNOWLEDGEMENTS

I want to thank the keepers of the words—the archivists, oral history recorders, museum curators, historical society members—all of whom sit in quiet places and make sure we don't lose our past and who know where to find it. I am so entirely grateful to all those who sat down with me to share their stories for this book, even those who aren't in these pages but are still living in my heart.

Kay Harper, who sat and talked with me for hours in Los Alamos, with her wisdom and knowledge; my dear friend Jana Benad Cowen, who drove me around northern New Mexico for a day and encouraged my exhausted adventure; my childhood friend Neteri Celena Johnston, whose mother, Betty, saw the Trinity blast; another dear friend Amy Rivers, who inspires me so much with her literary perseverance and talent; Donna Blake Birchell, who showed me this is possible; Joan Price, whose quirky persistence always encourages me to see things with a different slant; and my mother, Helgi, and my sister, Jennifer, who always have my back, read whatever I ask them to read and give me words to use when I run out.

Introduction

THE BALANCE OF TRUTH

The setting is World War II. The United States is about patriotism and support. The excitement of discovery is rampant for the scientists and soldiers involved at Los Alamos developing the bomb to end all war. But here, in the Tularosa Basin, the Jornada del Muerto and the Rio Grande Valley, the population is sparse, but the residents are a proud tough folk, many working as ranchers managing their cattle and other animals, prying a living out of the desert. It is these people who were displaced from their homes and never told what was coming. Here is the story of the first atomic bomb in the world, from those who were here to be part of this history.

This book is about experience—human remembered experience.

What that means is that it isn't always going to fit into known facts. People experience and remember things differently. And to make matters worse, those memories get transmitted in second- and third-hand ways, sometimes to the point that they don't even make sense.

For example, in a written account found at the Tularosa Basin Historical Museum, John Buckner wrote, "Helen Keller and her companion were traveling across the southern part of the state and when the light went over, she turned to her friend and said, 'What was that?' To anyone, not familiar with her, she was totally blind."

Helen Keller was a lot of things—deaf-blind author, political activist and lecturer. But she was not in a car driving through southern New Mexico at 5:35 a.m. on July 16, 1945. There was, however, an eighteen-year-old woman, Georgia Green, who was in a car with her brother-in-law Joe

Wills on their way to Albuquerque from Socorro for an 8:00 a.m. music class. Green was blind, although she could perceive a little light and dark distinction, and reportedly saw the bright light at that time. Green's sister Elizabeth Ingram was also in the car and said, "We saw this great big flash of light, and my sister, she said, 'What happened?' It seemed like it lit up the whole prairie all around us."

So, there are accounts of strange things here—from the point of view of various realities—and the reader should take each on its own merit and suspend an expectation of perfect facts in favor of a more subjective reality. Even official and news accounts can be mistaken and skewed.

Author and historian Jim Eckles worked for many years at the public affairs office at White Sands Missile Range. In his book *Trinity: The History of an Atomic Bomb National Historic Landmark*, he writes about some of the misconceptions and misinformation he encountered during his years there: "Over the years we in Public Affairs worked hard to present factual information about Trinity Site and its history. If we made mistakes, we corrected them. However, correcting other people's mistakes proved pretty much impossible."

Some common misconceptions Eckles has come across in relation to the Trinity Test and Site:

- Radiation at the site will fog the film in a film camera. (It won't.)
- The bomb, plutonium based, has been thought to be uranium based.
- The gypsum white sand is a result of the bomb test. (It is not.)
- Roadblocks along U.S. Highway 70 during the 1950s were for atomic bomb tests on the missile range. (The Trinity Test is the only atomic bomb test ever held in the area of White Sands Missile Range.)
- Visitors at the site are heard explaining to family or friends that Jumbo is the bomb casing. "This error seems a bit remarkable," Eckles wrote, "when these same people seem astounded that the Schmidt/McDonald ranch house survived the explosion. To them an atomic explosion is so big it destroys everything for miles and miles."

Eckles has said he has had a constant battle with people who think the test took place in the Tularosa Basin, when in fact it did not. The Trinity Site is in the Jornada del Muerto (Journey of Death) to the west of the Oscuro

Jumbo was meant to enclose the atomic bomb to retain its precious plutonium, should it fail to properly detonate. The government later decided to not use the casing, and it was simply hoisted in a tower near the bomb test. It survived the detonation and remains at the Trinity Site to this day. *Photo by Elva K. Österreich, 2019.*

Mountains, and to get there from the Alamogordo side, you travel through Mockingbird Gap in the Oscuros.

Sometimes people get their memories confused with later nuclear tests and things they have read in the intervening years. For example, Warren Harding Gillie told an oral history interviewer, "They had houses built, brand-new homes, before this was blown up. And you couldn't find a stick o' wood big enough to use as a toothpick. And they put dummies in there, in there to see what would happen to them. They never found them either." While there were houses and dummies used in subsequent bomb tests in other states, there was nothing like that used during the Trinity Test.

One misconception has been that there were soldiers taken to the site on a train and forced to observe the blast from closed-in trenches, or variations on that idea. While this may have happened at one or more of the subsequent nuclear explosion tests held across the country, Eckles is certain it never happened here. Yet there are several secondhand accounts along those lines.

Commercial flight crews have sometimes been known to announce to their passengers that they could see Ground Zero below them. But the airspace

Miles of desert separate the site where the first atomic bomb was assembled, the Schmidt/McDonald ranch house, from the rest of the world. The Oscuro Mountains to the east provide a backdrop to the site. *Photo by Elva K. Österreich, 2019.*

above WSMR is off-limits to commercial aircraft. Eckles himself had such an experience: "I was on a commercial flight where the crew pointed out what they thought was GZ to the east of the airplane," he wrote. "What they pointed out was a warhead impact target area on the west edge of White Sands. The target area is graded regularly, so it is barren sand. It shows up very well against the surrounding grasslands."

Eckles said one of his favorite stories about the Trinity Site came from a man named Mark Harp, who sent him a packet of information "a while back," involving a hollow earth theory. Harp apparently believed there is a humanoid civilization living inside the earth. He believed the Trinity Site explosion shook the whole earth, and the humanoids were disturbed and concerned by the event. They thought there might be some kind of danger approaching, so they sent a team out of a hole at the North Pole in a flying ship to New Mexico to see what was going on. Unfortunately, their vehicle malfunctioned, and in July 1947, they crashed into the New Mexico desert northeast of Trinity Site, creating the alien confusion known as the Roswell incident.

And, just getting weirder, in an article titled "From Trinity to Crossroads: Folklore of the First Atomic Bomb Tests" in *Folklife Magazine*, James Deutsch said there are also mysterious legends about the significance of the number thirty-three in the tests.

"The site of the Trinity test is on the 33rd line of latitude north; the Japanese cities of Hiroshima and Nagasaki straddle the 33rd parallel; and their destruction was authorized by Harry S. Truman, the 33rd president of the United States, who was also a 33-degree Freemason," Deutsch wrote.

Finally, there are accounts from prominent community members about a school bus that took a field trip to Trinity Site shortly after the test. Eckles is certain that there is no way this could have happened at all, given the state of security at the site following the test. However, before he died in 2012, I heard the tale from Aubrey Dunn Sr., a fifteen-year New Mexico state senator who served for a time as the chairman of the state senate Finance

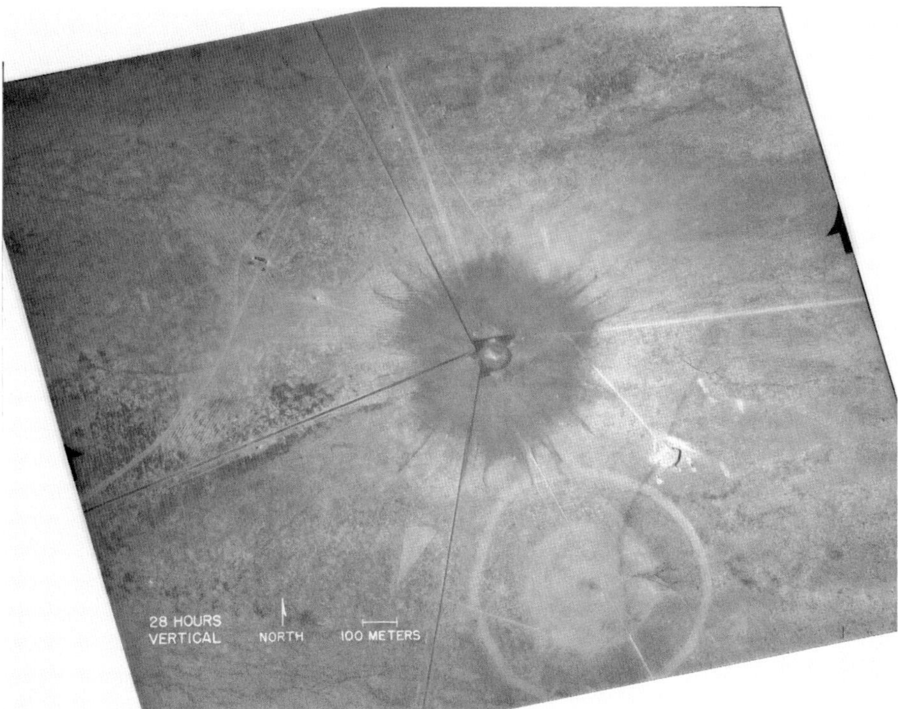

An aerial photo taken at Ground Zero twenty-eight hours after the explosion helped scientists determine the size of the crater left by the Trinity blast. The smaller crater to the southeast is from the earlier detonation of one hundred tons of TNT on May 7, 1945. The dark straight lines are roads. To the left of the crater is the Jumbo container, unharmed, and its collapsed tower (vertical line). *Photo courtesy Los Alamos National Laboratories.*

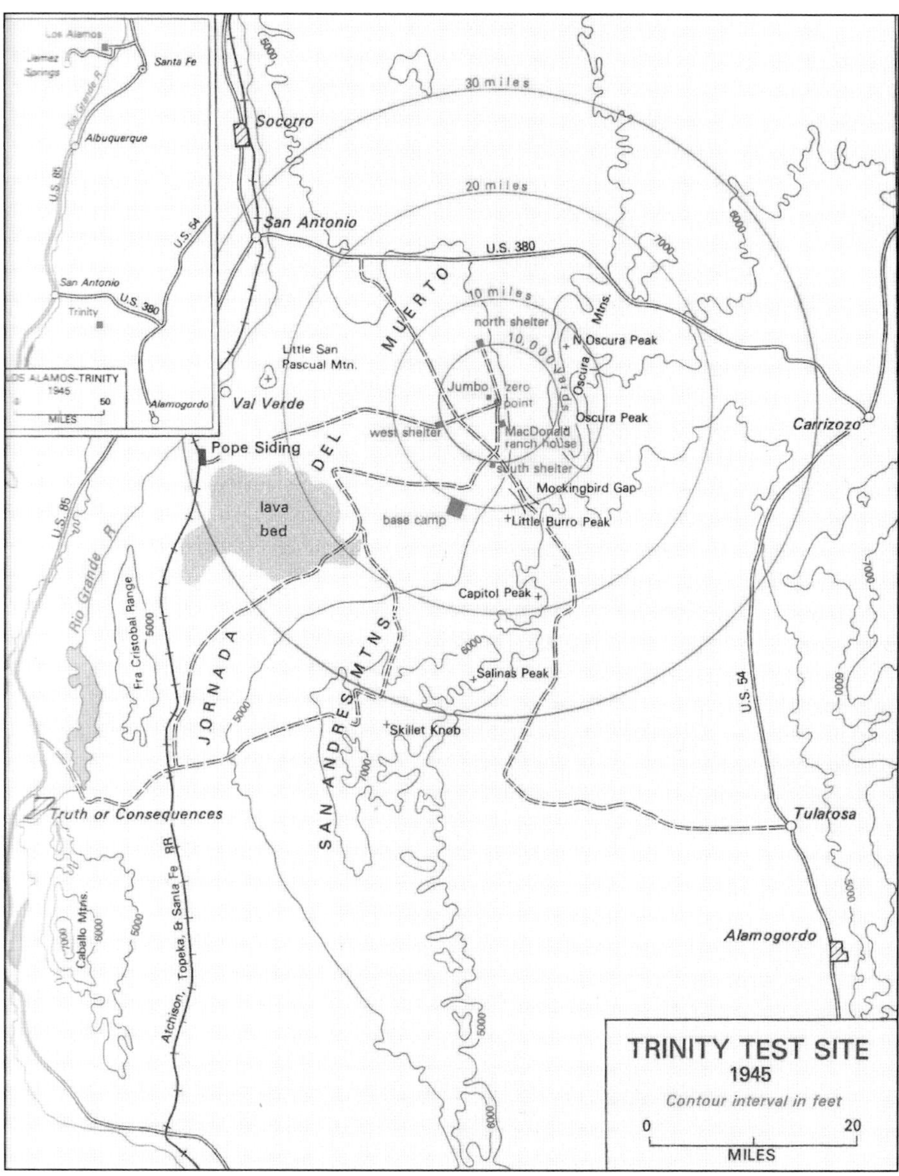

This map pinpoints the location of the Trinity Site in southern New Mexico. Many of the landmarks mentioned in this book can be found in this image. *Courtesy of the United States Army.*

Committee. Dunn, who was born in 1928, told me that he was on that school bus trip and was unimpressed by what he saw there.

Another Alamogordo resident, Betty Stoots, born in 1932, spoke to *Alamogordo Daily News* reporter Michael Shinabery in 2005. Stoots, according to the article, was on that bus "a day or two" after the Trinity test. "Everybody went up there and tromped all over the hot ground," she said. "Nobody really knew how dangerous it was. Nobody brought any of the dirt home. We didn't go down into the little crater, but all of the dust blew out just hotter than it could be. We were told to stay out of that because the government might want to inspect it. And we looked around at nothing. Piles of dirt. We were very unimpressed. It wasn't much fun."

Stoots said five adults accompanied them: Harold Hightower; Kenneth Bender, a teacher; her aunt and uncle, Frankie and Charlie Dean; and her mother. Later, she saw cattle that had been birthed in the blast radius. "They weren't malformed, but they'd turned kind of whitish," she said. "They put them in Alameda Park, and the kids could pet them. We all felt sorry for the little calves because they were in the bomb blast."

So, the remembrances here offer a subjective kind of truth. They are the memories and accounts of participants who viewed things through various lenses—not only the literal assortments of welding masks and photo films but also through the political and personal overlay of years since the original experience.

1

WHAT HAPPENED

The United States detonated the world's first atomic bomb at Trinity Site in the southern New Mexico desert at 5:29:45 a.m. Mountain Time on July 16, 1945.

The detonation was the culmination of the top-secret Manhattan Project, the goal of which was to build and deploy atomic weapons to bring about the end of World War II.

Army general Leslie R. Groves was commander over the project, leading the world into the atomic age.

A letter to President Franklin Roosevelt, sent in 1939 by Albert Einstein (written by Leo Szilárd and signed by Einstein), led to the development of the Manhattan Project. Einstein's letter convinced the president of the need to develop nuclear weapons before the Germans could do so. Other countries had already begun research on an atomic bomb. The atom had been split for the first time in 1938 in a Berlin laboratory, and nuclear fission was understood by the world's scientists.

> *In the course of the last four months it has been made probable—through the work of Joliot in France as well as Fermi and Szilárd in America—that it may become possible to set up a nuclear chain reaction in a large mass of uranium, by which vast amounts of power and large quantities of new radium-like elements would be generated. Now it appears almost certain that this could be achieved in the immediate future.*

Statues of J. Robert Oppenheimer and General Leslie Groves stand immortalized outside of the Los Alamos Public Library. Groves, with the Army Corps of Engineers, was a West Point graduate and led the top-secret effort to build the atomic bomb. Before being promoted to direct the Manhattan Project sites, he supervised construction of the Pentagon. *Photo by Elva K. Österreich, 2019.*

This new phenomenon would also lead to the construction of bombs, and it is conceivable—though much less certain—that extremely powerful bombs of a new type may thus be constructed. A single bomb of this type, carried by boat and exploded in a port, might very well destroy the whole port together with some of the surrounding territory. However, such bombs might very well prove to be too heavy for transportation by air.

I understand that Germany has actually stopped the sale of uranium from the Czechoslovakian mines which she has taken over. That she should have taken such early action might perhaps be understood on the ground that the son of the German Under-Secretary of State, von Weizsäcker, is attached to the Kaiser-Wilhelm-Institut in Berlin where some of the American work on uranium is now being repeated.

—excerpts from the Einstein letter

Thus, the Manhattan Project took shape, and Enrico Fermi and his colleagues produced the world's first sustained nuclear reaction at the University of Chicago's Metallurgical Laboratory in 1942. The technology for producing fissionable material for anything greater than a laboratory scale was unknown, so scientists had to find the pathway to large-scale atomic use. Two fissionable materials were considered: uranium-235 and plutonium-239. Scientists at the University of California at Berkeley, Columbia University and a secret organization in New York carried out research on separating the isotope U-235 from the naturally occurring element U-238. The University of Chicago was conducting research on plutonium at the same time.

When the Manhattan Project was beginning, then graduate student Richard Feynman was one of those asked to participate—to throw his hat in the rapidly expanding ring of scientists, even at his desk at college. He said he wasn't going to do it, but then as he tried to focus on his studies, he realized it was something he had to do.

"I said 'I'm not going to do it,'" he said in a 1975 lecture at the University of California–Santa Barbara. "The Germans had Hitler, and the possibility of developing an atomic bomb was obvious, and the possibility that they would develop it before we did was very much of a fright." He was invited to a secret meeting held at 3:00 p.m. "By four o'clock, I already had a desk in a room."

From 1943 to 1944, a facility for the separation of U-235 was constructed at Oak Ridge, Tennessee. It had two sites, one for separation by the electromagnetic process and one for separation by gaseous, later thermal, diffusion. The Oak Ridge facility covered fifty-four acres of land and, at its peak in May 1945, employed eighty-two thousand people. At the same time, a huge industrial complex was constructed in Hanford, Washington, for plutonium production. It occupied a six-hundred-square-mile site and employed more than forty-five thousand people.

Meanwhile, in Los Alamos, New Mexico, a secret scientific laboratory was established under the direction of J. Robert Oppenheimer. The purpose of this facility was to design and assemble the actual uranium- and plutonium-base atomic weapons. A prominent private ranch school for boys, Los Alamos Ranch School was the site selected in late 1942 by Oppenheimer, and as the school became a thing of the past, Los Alamos became a top-secret city. The first contingent of scientists arrived in March 1943. By June, 250 scientific personnel were at work on the physical, chemical and metallurgical aspects of the bomb's development. Two dozen scientists who had been performing related work in Britain, including Neils Bohr, joined in the Los Alamos

Left: Enrico Fermi, Italian-born physicist, received the 1938 Nobel Prize in physics. *Photo courtesy of the U.S. Department of Energy.*

Below: One of the Bathtub Row houses in Los Alamos serves as a museum preserving the sense of time and place experienced by the scientists from around the world who found themselves sequestered in a secret town to develop a secret project, the atomic bomb. *Photo by Elva K. Österreich, 2019.*

effort under a secret agreement between Roosevelt and Winston Churchill, Britain's prime minister. Before all was said and done, there were more than 2,500 people working at Los Alamos.

In 1944, scientists began to look for a type of detonation assembly that was not configured like a gun because the characteristics of plutonium precluded the ability of a gun-type mechanism to react fast enough. This reorganization of thought led to a more technically difficult detonation technique, implosion.

The implosion method involved surrounding a sub-critical sphere of plutonium with high explosives that would, when detonated, uniformly compress the plutonium into a supercritical mass in a few millionths of a second. The mechanics of creating such an implosion with the necessary degree of speed and accuracy were untried and extremely difficult to perfect.

While work continued with a gun-type assembly for the uranium bomb, the plutonium bomb would have to be tested before being used in combat. There were too many unknowns about the implosion device to take a risk of failure. It was decided that an atomic test would alleviate the fear of having it fall into enemy hands and provide quantitative data on a nuclear explosion that could be collected in no other way.

The site for such a test had to be isolated, have good weather conditions and relatively level terrain and be within a day's drive of Los Alamos. After looking at eight potential sites, officials chose an eighteen-by-twenty-four-mile section of the northwest corner of the Second Air Force's Alamogordo Bombing Range (now part of the White Sands Missile Range). Located in what is known as the Jornada del Muerto, the site is just north of the San Andreas Mountains and several miles west of the Oscura Mountains. It is flat, desolate and semiarid.

Oppenheimer gave the area the code name "Trinity," reportedly inspired by a poem by John Donne called "Holy Sonnet XIV: Batter My Heart, Three-Personed God," which begins:

Batter my heart, three-personed God; for you
As yet but knock, breathe, shine, and seek to mend;
That I may rise and stand, o'erthrow me, and bend
Your force to break, blow, burn, and make me new.

Once the test site was chosen, site preparations proceeded rapidly. An area was designated as Ground Zero, and things started moving. Field instruments, structures, bunkers and a firing station were erected.

The New Mexico desert on the Jornado del Muerto has changed little since the atomic bomb explosion at the Trinity Site. *Photo by Elva K. Österreich, 2019.*

Just a fraction of the thousands of feet of wire and cable stretched around the Trinity Site during the setup for the test. *Photo courtesy of the U.S. Department of Energy.*

One of the original windmills at the Schmidt/McDonald ranch house is still visible. The San Andreas Mountains are in the background. *Photo by Elva K. Österreich, 2019.*

Administrative and living quarters for test personnel were assembled at the former McDonald brothers ranch nine miles southwest of Ground Zero. When the army took possession of the McDonald Ranch in 1944, it was a working ranch with several structures, including two ranch houses, several outbuildings, an earthen reservoir, several windmills and a water tank.

By the time of the test, about 325 personnel were housed at the site and surrounding areas, including 250 Los Alamos scientists and support staff, 30 Special Engineer Detachment (SED) personnel, and 45 military policemen.

Hope Snow (now Evans) was a teenager growing up in the town of Carrizozo as scientists and other personnel prepared for the atomic test. Her parents ran the Malpais Courts, a tourist motel. She remembers that some of the scientists stayed at the courts:

> *My folks had that tourist court, some of the scientists that were working on the Manhattan Project stayed there. These scientists lived not just in my dad's tourist court but there was another one. There were about fifteen* [scientists] *there, in Carrizozo. They did not mingle with the people in Carrizozo, but they were friendly. As a teenager, I didn't pay attention, but*

Hope Evans at her Alamogordo home in 2019. Hope grew up in Carrizozo and lived with her parents, who owned a little tourist court (motel) at the time of the Trinity Test. *Photo by Elva K. Österreich, 2019.*

> *my folks said they knew they were there for some big project, but they never talked about it.*
>
> *They had been there maybe a month and would go out to the range to work and then come in at night. The night before the bomb went off, we had had a big rainstorm. My dad said they were all so muddy when they come in. In the bunker, I guess was mud.*
>
> *Anyway, they were so delighted, so he* [her father] *knew when they told everybody in town there had been a big explosion that it was more than that. They said there was an explosion on the railroad. Well they* [her parents] *knew better than that. All they told my dad was that this was going to make a difference in the end of the war situation, and of course, it did. It was only about another month or so until it was over. I do know it took a while before people knew what it was.*

Living at the Trinity Site could be an adventure at times, as the people there lived their day-to-day existences. Military policeman (MP) Marvin Davis Sr. was assigned to the Trinity site on December 30, 1944, and remained there through the test. He wrote a series of letters in the mid-1980s to the White Sands Missile Range public affairs office, which Jim Eckles printed as an appendix in his book *Trinity: The History of an Atomic Bomb National Historic Landmark.*

Davis and the other MPs relied on horses for some of their work and much of their recreation, playing polo and hunting when not on the clock. They shot antelope and mule deer on their trips, which were then served in the mess hall on-site. They also joined the scientists and other residents in some rousing volleyball games.

"In the evenings, we played a lot of volleyball—we had the net stretched between the latrine and our barracks," Davis wrote. "I wonder what people would think of volleyball teams with names like Enrico Fermi, George Kistiakowsky, Norris Bradbury on them. They were all glad to relax in the evening and get their minds off their work."

Supplies and services were provided out of the town of Socorro to the west, where Davis wrote about traveling to fetch water (that at the site was too alkaline to drink), pick up gasoline and get mail. "We could make the mail run and get a haircut at the shop in town. Sometimes we got so shaggy, we had to use the horse clippers to trim our hair up and they were about a foot long with a head about 4 inches wide."

Davis was there when the test took place about ten miles away. He wore a film badge to register the radiation he might have been absorbing and

Marvin Davis and two of the military police horses, Argo and Peergo. *Photo courtesy of Marvin Davis; provided by Jim Eckles.*

was given an arch welders' glass to watch through. "I was told to look at an oblique angle instead of straight at it. We had them [the welders' glass] taped in a cardboard shield. I still couldn't keep my eyes open and the heat was like opening up an oven door, even at 10 miles. I often wonder if any of the men suffered from radiation. I don't think I had any effects, but all I did was to take the men to their posts when the guards were posted. I didn't stay too long around Zero Point."

Eckles notes in his book that Davis lived a long and full life, dying at the age of eighty-seven on October 22, 2009.

Jumbo

Meanwhile, in March 1944, Oppenheimer requested the construction of a "sphere for proof firing" the implosion-type plutonium bomb. At that time, work on the implosion device was encountering great difficulty, and scientists wanted a means of recovering the bomb's plutonium-239, in scarce supply, in the event of a test failure. Jumbo was conceived as the answer. It was an enormous steel container in which the bomb could be detonated.

Opposite: There are no photos of Jumbo being manufactured. The first images made of Jumbo are as it arrives at the Pope, New Mexico siding just west of Trinity Site. Here workers are preparing to roll it off the railcar onto a platform, which they will then jack up and roll a huge trailer under. *Photo courtesy of Los Alamos National Laboratories.*

Above: Workers pose in front of Jumbo on its special trailer. *Photo courtesy of New Mexico State University Library, Archives and Special Collections.*

Specifications required that it completely contain the force of the bomb's high explosives and permit the mechanical and chemical recovery of the bomb's unexploded plutonium.

It took more than thirteen months to design, build and install Jumbo at the test site. By then, Los Alamos scientists were confident that the implosion device would work, and the decision was made to conduct a conventional, open-air test. Jumbo was made ready anyway in the event of a last-minute test change.

Jumbo was a 214-ton cast steel cylinder that was twenty-five feet long and ten feet in diameter. Built by the Babcock and Wilcox Company in Berberton, Ohio, Jumbo was shipped from Ohio to New Mexico on a specially built flatcar along a roundabout route that avoided bridges and tunnels too small to accommodate its huge bulk. When it arrived at a rail siding in Pope, New Mexico, in May 1945, it was towed by Army D7 bulldozers twenty-eight

Herbert Lehr and Haroutune Krikor "Harry" Daghlian Jr. load the assembled tamper plug containing the plutonium pit and initiator into a sedan for transport from the Schmidt/McDonald ranch house to the shot tower on July 13, 1945. Daghlian died on September 15, 1945, because he accidentally irradiated himself during an experiment in August at Los Alamos. *Photo courtesy Los Alamos National Laboratories.*

miles across a new road made just for this transport in the desert to a site eight hundred yards northeast of Ground Zero in a sixty-four-wheel trailer.

A sixty-foot-tall steel tower, eighteen feet at the base constructed of I-beam sections, and Jumbo were hoisted long-wise into the air and set into place. There, the weighty vessel survived the July 16 explosion, eight hundred feet to the southeast, completely intact.

GROUND ZERO, ZERO HOUR

From this crude la that spawned a dud, la?
Their necks to Truman's axe uncurled.
Lo, the embattled savants stood
An fired the flop heard 'round the world.
—popular parody circulated among Trinity Site technicians before the test.

At Ground Zero, a 102-foot tower was erected, about 25 feet square at the bottom and 15 feet square at the top platform. Completed in mid-June 1945, dry-run tests began in early July. On the evening of July 13, the bomb's high

A replica of the Gadget housed at the National Museum of Nuclear Science & History in Albuquerque, New Mexico, gives visitors a feel of the size and complexity of the casing that housed the atomic bomb set off at the Trinity Site on July 16, 1945. *Photo by Elva K. Österreich, 2019.*

The Gadget is hoisted to the top of the tower on July 14, 1945. The two large coaxial cables stretching down and toward the right may have ultimately caused the red color in some of the trinitite found later. *Photo courtesy Los Alamos National Laboratories.*

explosive assembly arrived from Los Alamos at noon. The bomb, nicknamed the Gadget, was assembled.

At 4:45 a.m. on July 16, an arming party closed the arming switches at the base of the tower. This was the last visit to Ground Zero before the test.

Some even thought that the Trinity test might "ignite" the earth's atmosphere, eliminating all life on the planet. Less wild estimates thought that New Mexico might be incinerated. Yet they flipped the switch on the test.

At 5:29:45 a.m., the world's first atomic bomb was detonated with the force of approximately twenty-one kilotons of TNT above the desert of southern New Mexico.

> *We were twenty miles away, others were closer, six miles away, they gave out dark glasses. I thought, "I ain't going to see a damn thing through dark glasses." The only thing that can really hurt your eyes is the ultraviolet*

The atomic age begins in the early morning on July 16, 1945. *Photo courtesy Los Alamos National Laboratories.*

light. So, I got behind a truck windshield so the ultraviolet can't go through glass and that would be safe and so I could see the damn thing.

The time comes, and there was this tremendous flash out there. It was so bright. And I see this purple splotch on the floor of the truck, and I said, "That ain't it, that's an after image," and I look up. I see this white light, changing into yellow then to orange. The clouds form, and then they disappear again. The compression and the expansion forms and makes clouds disappear. Finally, a big ball of orange at the center so bright it became a wall of orange started to rise and billow a little bit and get black around the edges, and then you see it's a big ball of smoke with flashes inside with fire going.

And I saw all that took about one minute—a series from bright to dark, and I had seen it. I'm about the only guy in the world who actually looked at the damn thing. Everybody else had dark glasses. The people at six miles couldn't see it because they are all told to lie the floor. I'm the only guy who saw it with the human eye.

Finally, after about a minute and a half, suddenly there is a tremendous noise, bang and then rumbles like thunder, and that's what convinced me. Nobody had said a word during this whole minute, we all were just watching quietly, but this sound released everybody, released me in particular. Because the solidity of the sound at that distance meant that it really worked. The man who was standing next to me asked, "What's that?" when the sound went off. I said, "That was the bomb."

—Richard Feynman, 1975 UCSB lecture

2

THE FIRST DAY

Trinity Site

5:30 a.m. on July 16, 1945

And just at that instant there rose
from the bowels of the earth
a light not of this world,
the light of many suns in one.
—William L. Laurence

In his book *You Take the Sundials and Give Me the Sun*, Tularosa Basin historian David Townsend makes the point that it is the people who saw the atomic bomb first who are rarely asked if they were victims. "Few of them would consider themselves victims, yet in a broad sense they were. They were located in close proximity to a dangerous experiment; not informed of the danger in which they were being placed, let alone the nature of the experiment; and deceived for a period of weeks about the danger in which they had been placed," Townsend wrote.

Although he interviewed a number of those who experienced the Trinity Test, in his book, Townsend doesn't name them but puts the experiences together and talks about them, with one exception. He recounts his experience with Clara Snow.

He conducted an interview with Snow on May 13, 1975, at her home in Carrizozo. When he asked her if she had witnessed the bomb, her reaction was "stunning, emotional, a combination of fear, anger and bitterness that led her to tears."

"It was as if the air had died," Snow told Townsend.

Most of his sources did not notice much unusual activity prior to July 16, 1945. The people of Carrizozo, a railroad town, were used to heavy movement of men and equipment as the war still raged in the Pacific. Some who were interviewed were convinced there was unusually heavy truck traffic at the time. Snow told Townsend that the government was moving a huge amount of garden hose somewhere. Union Pacific men had heard about some unusual equipment being moved on the Santa Fe through Socorro. Townsend wrote that official records reflect a frenzy of activity from July 12 to July 16, "but mostly in the Stallion Range area, across the Basin from Carrizozo."

One of the interviewed witnesses had to go to the Trinity Site to move some equipment and knew "something was up" because of the tense atmosphere. "He saw a tower with what looked like a 'little black pot hanging out on an arm of it,'" Townsend wrote. "When he asked about it, he was told simply that it would not be there when he came back."

Since the bomb went off at 5:25:45 a.m., the sources who remember the experience were "early risers, readying for work, cooking breakfast, or had been up all night nursing a sick child." Townsend continued:

> *They remember the light above all else, above the noise, above the tremors, above everything. One minute it was dark; then it was bright as day. The light faded gradually into what seemed a deeper darkness. Then the sound, not much noisier than distant thunder, and the tremor that rattled windows and dishes. The first thoughts were religious: the end of the world; the next, practical and reflective of wartime thoughts: they have sabotaged the train, or blown up the base, or.... Those who went outside to see what had happened were treated—or condemned—to a view never seen before by man. A giant column of smoke with light gradually dying down its stem was visible in the re-gathering darkness. As this false dawn was dying in the west, the true dawn was giving a hint of a purer light from the east. That picture stuck in the minds of the witnesses, indelibly imprinted.*
>
> *Then the silence came—an eerie silence where it seemed the air had died.*

Another interviewer, Howard Tate, spoke to a man who was in a remote location at the time, closer to the Trinity Site than to Carrizozo. The man said he was lying in bed under a sheet in a room with windows open. The curtains were moving gently in the breeze. Suddenly, it was daylight, and the sheet and curtain were blown in one direction. Then it was dark, and the sheet and curtains were sucked back in the other direction. Townsend said that sucking behavior may explain the silence reported by other witnesses.

The following are accounts from people who witnessed, first- or secondhand (through the recollections of parents or others), the occasion of the Trinity Ground Zero explosion.

Flora Millfelt

Flora Millfelt saw the Trinity explosion from the banks of the Rio Grande. Her family owned a ranch along the river near San Antonio, New Mexico, and while most people in the area were not told about the test, her father had been instructed to move some of his animals away from their grazing areas, so he took his family out to watch.

> *We went and watched it, my mother and all of us kids along the river. And it was five o'clock in the morning, and it was supposed to be dark, but it was just brighter than daylight. It looked like it was a ball of cotton coming up, you know. It was red. We were about a half a mile away.*

Flora Millfelt during a change of command event at White Sands Missile Range. Flora observed the Trinity explosion with her siblings on the banks of the Rio Grande near her father's ranch. *Photo by Elva K. Österreich, 2019.*

> *There were fourteen of us kids. Father knew about the bomb because they told him to move his cattle and sheep and goats. We got along the river; my dad got the information. We knew exactly where to go to watch. And we just saw this red cloud comes up, then it turns orange then it turns yellow then a boom, and it was brown and clear up in the air and everything was just as light as day.*
>
> *We weren't watching for radiation or anything like that; we didn't know about that. We had six doctors that were partners with us in 2002. I came up with breast cancer and was talking to him about it. He says 99 percent of my patients of people with breast cancer* [at his Albuquerque practice] *were people that were there when the atomic bomb went off. Most of my family died of some kind of cancer.*
>
> *I still have the ranch. It's an old Spanish grant. It's been in the family for generations, since the 1600s or so. It is in Los Torriones, right on Bosquicito Road. The ranch borders fourteen sections of BLM* [Bureau of Land Management] *land that borders the missile range. I rent the ranch out.*

HOLM BURSUM III

Holm Olaf Bursum III was a third-generation White Sands Missile Range rancher. During his childhood, he lived at Ozanne, a former stage stop in the 200,000-acre ranch his grandfather had amassed by buying up area homesteads, beginning in the 1890s. The ranch was approximately thirty-two miles long from east to west and ten miles wide from north to south. It was roughly bisected east to west by U.S. Highway 380. In 1942, the federal government required the southern half of the Bursum ranch for military testing.

Bursum recalled:

> *I was really the only one on the ranch at that time, in August of 1945. My mother and father and my little brother lived in town. When they set that off, I was at the Adobe Ranch, about eighteen miles north northeast of Trinity Site. I think they were supposed to set it off around midnight, and I think it rained that night and delayed it, so they set it off about 4:30 in the morning. It woke us up there at the Adobe....I was sleeping on the top deck of a double-decker bunk bed, and it rocked that bed enough that it woke me up.*

It was real bright, but in the wrong direction, 'cause my bed was next to a south window. That was the wrong way for the sun to come up, but it looked like the sun was coming up. It shook the house, and I remember there were cases of cans that were used for canning in the house, just empty cans that had not been used yet, new cans. I remember that it really rattled those cans. It was kind of a strange sound. The highway, Highway 380, was blocked off, and there was no traffic. I don't know for how long, but I guess it didn't make any difference—we weren't going anywhere, anyway. There was lots of army traffic on that highway.

The View from Bingham

The tiny town of Bingham is just twenty miles north of the Trinity Site. On the Trinity explosion's twenty-fifth anniversary, postmaster Harold Dean spoke with Associated Press science writer Bill Stockton.

"Has it really been twenty-five years?" Dean asked. On the day of the test, Dean was asleep in the rear of his store. He had kept it open late two nights in a row to accommodate lonely soldiers bivouacked nearby. Dean didn't know the soldiers were there to evacuate isolated ranches if need be.

"It rained on and off through the night, and that rain hittin' the window put me into a deep sleep," he said. "Then all of a sudden came the loudest bang I've ever heard. The first thing I remember is standing at the foot of the bed saying, 'Was that thunder?' but I knew it wasn't thunder. I was so tired I went back to bed. But I couldn't sleep. By then, it was light, so I got up and looked out. That's when I saw the cloud."

My View of the Atomic Bomb

By Floy "Bell" Di Risio

Floy "Bell" Di Risio's account was handwritten on August 8, 2000. It is in a file folder at the Tularosa Basin Historical Museum with no other information about her or why the account was collected. The account reads:

The Atomic bomb has been written about by many people from many walks of life from the presidents of the United States on down to the lowest technician who worked on it. This is a true story written by a young mother who by chance happend [sic] *to see the first Atomic Bomb light up our New Mexico skys* [sic]. *My middle son, in eleven days would be one year old, and I had gotten up to change his diaper! That of course was in the "olden days" when we used diaper pins. By accident I dropped one of the pins. The room was very dark and I didn't want to turn the light on for fear of waking my other son, who was two and one half years old. Suddenly a light came on in the room, it was so bright that I could see the delicate flowers in the wallpaper!*

At that time my dad was working for the city in the water department. On this early morning of July 16, 1945, he had gone up to the Alamo Canyon reservoir to check the water valves to be sure they were in working order. He came home about 8:30 a.m. to eat breakfast and he told my mother and I, that he had had quite an experience. He said that before daybreak he heard no sound but that he saw a light so bright that he could see the rock formations and crevases [sic] *in the San Andres Mountains. This was a distance of 40 or more miles. Then I told them my experience of finding the lost diaper pin in this bright light, we discussed it but not out of fear, we were just curious, but we came to no conclusion.*

In a week or two the Air Base released a bulletin that told us that an ammunition dump had blown up in a remote area of the base. Who were we to question our own Government? We were fighting a terrible war and were very patriotic. The base at that time was a bee-hive of activity, training B-17s, and if there was any extra activity we were not aware of it. After the news came out and we knew what really took place, my family never considered the fact that had anything gone wrong we would have been in danger. We simply trusted our Government. We believed that they were doing what had to be done to win the war, so our loved ones could come home.

I consider myself a very lucky person to have experienced history in the making. Before WWII life in Alamogordo was a typical small community. A place where you knew everyone and everyone was a good friend and neighbor to all. The "Bomb" changed my beautiful sleepy valley into a very technical metropolis. Over the next few years I never realized how much our valley had changed until I went to work in the Security department of the Ballistic Missile Branch at Holloman Air Force Base.

The Hereford cattle are common to our area and some of them, who were exposed to the blast were displayed in the park. They had gray blotches where the fallout had hit them, but they seemed no worse for the wear. We had friends who lived in the old Legitt-Myers mansion in the Black range near Hillsboro. They being ranchers were up early and saw the bright light and after daylight discovered a corner of their living room had a huge crack in it, running from top to bottom. These walls were made of two foot adobe, and the distance from the blast was close to 150 miles. My brother was in England in the hospital having been wounded in the "Battle of the Bulge." He was listening to the radio when the news came on mentioning Alamogordo, N.M. and the Atom Bomb. Of course he pictured it on the base not many miles uprange. He was one happy G.I. when he had mail from home saying all was well! In the end we will never know how many lives were lost or how many lives were saved by the Manhattan Project.

Memories of First A Bomb

By John Buckner

John Buckner's account is in a file folder at the Tularosa Basin Historical Museum with no other information about him, the date or why the account was collected. This account was clearly typed on a typewriter. It reads:

At this time we were living in Alamogordo, I was working for the Community Public Service Co. as service man and Lineman. The company was still operating the power plant across the tracks next to the sawmill. My duties consisted of maintaining the power lines in Alamogordo, Tularosa, La Luz and the line out to the air base.

The line crew was stationed in Silver City. Any major work on the lines they would come down to Alamo and take care of it. On the night before the bomb went off we had a very heavy rain and wind storm which broke down some lines and caused a lot of outages. A Mr. Bob Atkins (I believe that was his name) was working for the company also. He and I had been out all night, restoring power. We had everything back on the line except La Luz. We were checking that line, when I stuck my pickup in the mud, up over the running boards. We took our hooks and hand tools and walked into town and got another pickup.

The La Luz line branched off from the Tularosa line down next to the railroad tracks. I re-fused that line and had just reached the main highway, when this light traveled across, it held for a moment or so, just bright as day, then passed on by and faded out. It was interesting because you could just feel it as it went over.

I looked North West of Tularosa, there was a large column and spread of black and white smoke, among them were several shoots of flame up into them. Of all the pictures I have seen of this, none of them match what I remember seeing that morning.

We thought maybe a bomber had crashed up north which was happening fairly regular about that time. I turned around and drove to the overpass on the north side of Tularosa. The sky was clear and no sign of smoke. After returning to town, the base put out word that a powder magazine had blown up on upper range. That did not seem right to me. I decided due to the light possibly a meteorite had crashed.

The line crew got up early in Silver city, preparing to come down to do some work. They said they felt vibrations that shook the ground some and rattled windows. They assumed it was a tremor from an earthquake.

SILVER CLOUD SETTLES ON ALAMOGORDO

Excerpt from the Alamogordo Daily News, *Friday, July 15, 2005*

On July 15, 1945, 15-year-old Beatrice "Bea" Martinez and her friends went out to a dance as part of the feast of Our Lady of Mt. Carmel.

Following the dance, the group of friends decided to serenade all the Carmens they knew in honor of the feast day. They traveled around bringing Mañanitas to Carmen. When the group got to the house of Carmen Valle, who later became Martinez' sister-in-law, it was the wee hours of the morning of July 16. They were invited inside for hot chocolate and sweet bread.

"All of a sudden the house was engulfed in a luminous silver cloud, and we all ran out to see what had happened. All Alamogordo was under the silver cloud."

Everyone stood outside the Valle home waiting for whatever it was they had seen. It seemed a long time they waited, Bea said.

When the glow died down they went back in the house, finished their hot chocolate and went home.

"We never even asked what happened,' Bea said. "Since we did not know what it was all about we were not scared."

Later, after the atomic bomb was dropped in Japan, Bea and her friends went to the movies one day and, during the Movietone Newsreel before the feature, were surprised to see a short clip of Alamogordo's train depot at White Sands Boulevard and 10th Street. That was how they learned what the glow they had seen must have been.

Following the explosion, nine crews went in to record the aftermath. *Photo courtesy Los Alamos National Laboratories.*

"After the Japanese bombing we were surprised," Bea said. "They showed the scientists dressed in suits to protect them. We didn't hear any more until we started to hear in the papers what happened. That was the scary thing, that there was no warning."

JOE SAAVEDRA

Joe Saavedra's family has lived in Luis Lopez, a town between Socorro and San Antonio, for many years. His mother, Rachel Montoya, was born in the area in 1919. His dad, Ted, was also born in the area in 1916. The family had a view of the test from about twenty miles away. Rachel described the incident as "a really scary feeling."

> *During the war, when the bomb went off in 1945, they* [Rachel and her family] *said it turned night into day, early in the morning. They were*

about to get up. Everything shook, and they thought it was the end of the world. They didn't know what was going on. The government didn't say anything or anything. About a mile from here, in a little house back there, they all came running out, and they saw a big mushroom. It was four or five in the morning, and they were just amazed. They didn't know what was going on. They started praying. All of a sudden, the animals start to drop, cows and sheep. They were stunned, I guess, that's what my mom said. They just died. They changed color, and they were just dying because they were sheepherders back then, and some of their cows and chickens and horses and ducks fell down. It was creepy.

They weren't paid for their animals or anything. Nobody told them what was going on. Nobody ever asked them anything. People were to themselves when they were out here, you know. They weren't nosy, and the government was hush hush—don't say nothing. That's what happened back then.

Most died of cancer. My sister-in-law has cancer now too. Everybody around here has cancer. In Socorro County, there is a high rate of cancer.

Dogie lambs raised by Annie Gaines on the Gaines place, circa 1929–30. *Photo courtesy of Human Systems Research and White Sands Missile Range.*

Jess Gililland

Jess Gililland was fourteen at the time of the test and part of a ranching family. He was woken by the explosion, along with his brother and a cousin, who were all sleeping on the porch twenty-seven miles away from the blast.

"We were up on that slope where we had plain sight of that," Gililland said. "Didn't have no idea what it was. That mushroom smoke settled to the north [toward Bingham] We didn't see [the flash] because it was already over. When it woke us up we heard the sound."

Gilliland told the *Alamogordo Daily News* in 2005 that rancher Henry Jackson did see the flash. Jackson was outside working under the hood of his pickup, and he thought his wife walked up with a light because it got so bright, but then it got dark just as fast. It was later that Gilliland found out what the blast actually was. "They didn't tell us nothing," he said, and his wife added, "It was all top secret. They had wire strung all over the place."

"The piñons were all cream-colored that year instead of brown," Gilliland said.

Joy Means

When Joy Means was a little more than a month away from her fourth birthday, she awoke to the sound of distant thunder, she told an *Alamogordo Daily News* reporter in 2005. She went to a window in her family's Carrizozo home to watch the storm.

"I saw a blinding white light and the sky turned a pink color I had never seen before and hope to never see again," she said. "Mother was telling me to go back to bed, and I was telling her I wanted to look for the 'tater wagon.' When I saw the blinding white flash and everything turn pink, I was scared and wanted to jump back in bed….The house was shaking, the windows were rattling. Bob [Joy's teenage brother] was screaming, the bed was bouncing, dishes and canned good were breaking all over the kitchen."

Bob, who had just returned from the Philippines with a shattered ankle from a Japanese attack, had a cast from the tip of his toes to the top of his thigh. He was yelling, "Take cover! The Japs are attacking!" Her mom pushed the children under a bed and told them to stay next to the wall.

"Vestal [Joy's six-year-old brother] and I told her we couldn't find the wall because it was moving. I heard Bob loading rifles and hobbling through the house giving orders to my other brothers to guard different sides of the house. I remember when he gave mother a rifle, and he told her, 'Save a bullet for you and the kids. Don't let them take you alive.'"

When the house stopped shaking, Joy and Vestal found a box of apples, oranges and nuts in a box under the bed with them. "Vestal and I were mad because we were not given a gun to protect ourselves," Joy said. "We came up with a plan to throw fruit and nuts at the attackers. Looking back now, that wasn't the best tactical plan anyone ever devised, but we planned on going down fighting if we had to go down."

When the sun came up, Bob went to find out what happened. He told the family to stay completely still and quiet until he got back. When he got back, he said they could move around but had to stay close to the house. The town was told there was an explosion at the Alamogordo Bombing Range.

"Everyone in town knew the story of an ammo dump blowing up was not true," she said. "They wondered why they were being lied to by the military."

Joy said the event was a concern to the people of the area not because of fear of aftereffects but because everyone was going hungry. The canned jars were shattered. No one could buy groceries because the canned goods at the stores were shattered as well.

"Everyone was upset with the mess they had to clean up. We were more fortunate than most because we had fruit and nuts and Mother had several tin pie pans that we could eat out of since the dishes were broken."

Elizabeth McVeigh

Elizabeth McVeigh was seventeen when the light woke her up in Carrizozo that morning. "It was just strange," she said. "I woke up, and the light and everything was so different from anything I had ever seen before. Of course, we didn't know what it was. [There was shaking] like an explosion, but the light was all I remembered."

Years later, around 1955, McVeigh, her husband and her son joined a caravan to visit the Trinity Site. It was unfenced at that time. Trinitite was scattered about, and the visitors picked up the pieces. "Everybody was picking them up, and I was too," she said. Her son put some in his pocket, and they ended up in a cardboard box at their house. McVeigh links that trinitite to a cancer diagnosis she had in 1999.

"It amazes me that they didn't know enough about it to keep people away from it. They didn't have any idea how dangerous it was.…They didn't tell us. They didn't tell us. We were just in the dark about the whole thing."

Numerous interviews, stories and remembrances are recorded every year during the two open house days (held on the first Saturday of each April and October) at White Sands Missile Range when people can visit the site of the Trinity Explosion. *Photo by Elva K. Österreich, 2019.*

FAY LISK

The following account about Fay Lisk was printed in the *Las Cruces Bulletin* and in *Desert Exposure* in July 2020 and was written by the author.

> *Fay Lisk was 12 years old and fast asleep at 5:30 a.m., July 16, 1945, when her mother was outside doing something and saw a big flash in the sky. Their family lived on a ranch some 45 miles north of the place the Atomic Age began, now known as the Trinity Test Site.*
>
> *Fay said her mother-in-law lived in Mountainair, 75 miles as the crow flies, from Trinity Site, and she saw the windows shake like a big earthquake had hit her house. It wasn't until the United States dropped the bomb on Japan, August 6 and 9, 1945, that the people of the Tularosa Basin, Jornada del Muerto and surroundings knew what happened in their area of the world. Headlines screamed the U.S. had destroyed two cities, Hiroshima and Nagasaki, and the successful test in southern New Mexico was a back-page story.*

"It was after they bombed Japan that we found out that they set the test bomb off," said Fay, who was born in 1932 and now makes her home in Globe, Arizona. "Everything was such a secret, we knew there was a town of Los Alamos, but all the contact we actually had was a radio, and we would get a little news that way."

At Bingham, 20 miles north of Trinity Site, was the schoolhouse where Lisk went to school growing up. She stayed with Ted and Sylvia Myers during the school week. Ted and Christian Myers drove the two school buses that served the school. Fay graduated from 8th grade in May 1945.

"At the time, Bingham was on the old dirt road that went across there," she said. "There was a little post office and a little store and some little cabins. There was one teacher and that year I think we had 12–13 kids who went to school there. I was the only one in 8th grade. I loved school."

Living next to the Myers was a younger couple, the husband's name was Henry, Fay remembers. They would visit to play cards.

"He [Henry] *had a short scruffy black beard—all of a sudden he had these big blotches all over it," Fay said. "They were gray like if you had thrown bleach on somebody. And* [another family] *had ducks that hatched out deformed. There was just a lot of this that people started talking about. Cows and cats with blotches. They* [the government] *never did say or do anything about it."*

Fay went on to say the people who ran the Bingham store, Harold and Sally Dean died, she thinks, with lung cancers. The Myers moved to Farmington and suffered early deaths, although she didn't know why. Fay's mother died in 1970 from lung cancer.

As an adult visiting the United Nations building in New York Fay saw a display about the things that happened in Japan. She said it was truly terrible but the bombs ended the war and feels many more people would have died had the atomic bombs not been dropped.

"I think that if it hadn't had been for that, we would have lost a lot more Americans," she said. "And it ended the war. It ended—poof—right then."

3

ON-SITE

When the Trinity Test bomb was detonated, there were people stationed at various locations far and near for the purpose of watching and recording what they saw.

Bunkers were established ten thousand yards due north, west and south of the tower, known as N-10,000, W-10,000 and S-10,000. Each had its own shelter chief. Many other observers were around twenty miles away, and some others were scattered at different distances, some in more informal situations. Richard Feynman claimed to be the only person to see the explosion without the goggles provided, relying on a truck windshield to screen out harmful ultraviolet wavelengths.

Brigadier General Thomas F. Farrell described the scene inside the S-10,000 shelter with several of the primary scientists, including Oppenheimer. There were about twenty people in that space six miles from the explosion. Farrell was General Leslie R. Groves's deputy. His account was included in Groves's memorandum for the secretary of war on July 18, 1945.

"The scene inside the shelter was dramatic beyond words," Farrell wrote. For some two hours before the blast, Groves was at the shelter with Oppenheimer, who was restless and agitated, in a state of "tense excitement." Farrell continued:

> *Every time the Director* [Oppenheimer] *would be about to explode because of some untoward happening, General Groves would take him off and walk with him in the rain, counselling* [sic] *with him and reassuring*

Going in party following the Trinity Test at the N-10,000 bunker, part of the recovery/inspection team. *Photo courtesy Los Alamos National Laboratories.*

him that everything would be all right. At twenty minutes before zero hour, General Groves left for his station at the base camp, first because it provided a better observation point and second, because of our rule that he and I must not be together in situations where there is an element of danger, which existed at both points....

The tension increased by leaps and bounds. Everyone in that room knew the awful potentialities of the thing that they thought was about to happen. The scientists felt that their figuring must be right and that the bomb had to go off but there was in everyone's mind a strong measure of doubt.... We were reaching into the unknown and we did not know what might come of it. It can be safely said that most of those present—Christian, Jew, Athiest [sic]*—Were praying and praying harder than they had ever prayed before....*

In that brief instant in the remote New Mexico desert the tremendous effort of the brains and brawn of all these people came suddenly and startlingly to the fullest fruition. Dr. Oppenheimer, on whom had rested a very heavy burden, grew tenser as the last seconds ticked off. He scarcely breathed. He held on to a post to steady himself. For the last few seconds, he stared directly ahead and then when the announcer shouted "Now!" and there came a tremendous burst of light followed shortly thereafter by the deep growling roar of the explosion. His face relaxed into an expression of tremendous relief. Several of the observers standing back of the shelter to watch the lighting effects were knocked flat by the blast.

The following are firsthand accounts of scientists and technical personnel who were at and near the Trinity Site and knew what was going on.

Otto Frisch, 1904–1979

Otto Frisch was an Austrian-born British physicist who worked on nuclear physics. He was the leader of the Critical Assemblies group with the Manhattan Project. One of his tasks was to determine the exact amount of enriched uranium required to create the critical mass, the mass of uranium that would sustain a nuclear chain reaction. He returned to England in 1946 to take a position as head of the nuclear physics division of the Atomic Energy Research Establishment at Harwell and spent much of his time teaching at Cambridge. He retired in 1972 and died on September 22, 1979.

And then without a sound, the sun was shining; or so it looked. The sand hills at the edge of the desert were shimmering in a very bright light, almost colourless and shapeless. This light did not seem to change for a couple of seconds and then began to dim. I turned round, but that object on the horizon which looked like a small sun was still too bright to look at. I kept blinking and trying to take looks, and after another ten seconds or so it had grown and dimmed into something more like a huge oil fire with a structure that made it look a bit like a strawberry.

It was slowly rising into the sky from the ground, with which it remained connected by a lengthening stem of swirling dust incongruously, I thought of a red-hot elephant standing balanced on its trunk. Then, as the cloud of hot gas cooled and became less red, one could see a blue glow surrounding it, a glow of ionized air.…The object, now clearly what has become so well known as the mushroom cloud, ceased to rise but a second mushroom started to grow out from its top; the inner layers of the gas were kept hot by their radioactivity and, being hotter than the rest, broke through the top and rose to even greater height. It was an awesome spectacle; anybody who has ever seen an atomic explosion will never forget it. And all in complete silence; the bang came minutes later, quite loud though I had plugged my ears, and followed by a long rumble like heavy traffic very far away. I can still hear it.

Enrico Fermi, 1901–1954

Enrico Fermi, the Italian who had pioneered the first controlled nuclear chain reaction in December 1942, gazed over the desert on July 15 at "the world on the eve of its disintegration." The man who had opened a new world with the aid of his slide rule did not believe this would happen. He planned to shred bits of paper to measure the blast by how far the shock wave blew them.

On the morning of the 16th of July, I was stationed at the Base Camp at Trinity in a position about ten miles from the site of the explosion.

The explosion took place at about 5:30 a.m. I had my face protected by a large board in which a piece of dark welding glass had been inserted. My first impression of the explosion was the very intense flash of light, and a sensation of heat on the parts of my body that were exposed. Although I did not look directly towards the object, I had the impression that suddenly the countryside became brighter than in full daylight. I subsequently looked in the direction of the explosion through the dark glass and could see something that looked like a conglomeration of flames that promptly started rising. After a few seconds the rising flames lost their brightness and appeared as a huge pillar of smoke with an expanded head like a gigantic mushroom that rose rapidly beyond the clouds probably to a height of 30,000 feet. After reaching its full height, the smoke stayed stationary for a while before the wind started dissipating it. About 40 seconds after the explosion the air blast reached me. I tried to estimate its strength by dropping from about six feet small pieces of paper before, during, and after the passage of the blast wave. Since, at the time, there was no wind I could observe very distinctly and actually measure the displacement of the pieces of paper that were in the process of falling while the blast was passing. The shift was about 2½ meters, which, at the time, I estimated to correspond to the blast that would be produced by ten thousand tons of T.N.T.

The Nobel Prize–winning physicist Enrico Fermi at a blackboard. Fermi, born in Italy, created the first sustained nuclear reaction in a squash court at the University of Chicago on December 2, 1942. *Photo courtesy of the U.S. Department of Energy.*

Two tanks were used at Trinity Site on the day of the explosion and the next day to gather core and soil samples from the area. The one on the left was manned by Enrico Fermi and Herbert Anderson for obtaining soil samples from the crater shortly after the test. *Photo from Carl Rudder's scrapbook provided by Jim Eckles.*

Luis Alvarez, 1911–1988

In 1944, Luis Walter Alvarez arrived at Los Alamos to work on the Manhattan Project, where he devised an electrical detonation method for the plutonium bomb. He and his graduate student Lawrence Johnston also designed equipment to measure the energy released by a nuclear explosion. He was an American experimental physicist, inventor and professor and was eventually awarded the Nobel Prize in Physics in 1968. Alvarez died of cancer of the esophagus at the age of seventy-seven on September 1, 1988.

> *I was kneeling between the pilot and co-pilot in B-29 No. 384 and observed the explosion through the pilot's window on the left side of the plane. We were about 20 to 25 miles from the site and the cloud cover between us and the ground was approximately 7/10. About 30 seconds before the object was detonated the clouds obscured our vision of the point so that we did not see the initial stages of the ball of fire. I was looking through crossed Polaroid glasses directly at the site. My first sensation was one of intense light covering my whole field of vision. This seemed to last for about ½ second after which I noted an intense orange red glow through the clouds. Several seconds later it appeared that a second spherical red ball appeared but it is probable that this apparent phenomenon was caused by the motion*

of the airplane bringing us to a position where we could see through the cloud directly at the ball of fire which had been developing for the past few seconds. This fire ball seemed to have a rough texture with irregular black lines dividing the surface of the sphere into a large number of small patches of reddish orange. This thing disappeared a few seconds later and what seemed to be a third ball of fire appeared again and I am now convinced that this was all the same fire ball which I saw on two separate occasions through a new hole in the undercast.

When this "third ball" disappeared the light intensity dropped considerably and within another 20 seconds or so the cloud started to push up through the undercast. It first appeared as a parachute which was being blown up by a large electric fan. After the hemispherical cap had emerged through the cloud layer one could see a cloud of smoke about 1/3 the diameter of the "parachute" connecting the bottom of the hemisphere with the undercast. This had very much the appearance of a large mushroom. The hemispherical structure was creased with "longitude lines" running from the pole to the equator. In another minute the equatorial region had partially caught up with the poles giving a flattened out appearance to the top of the structure. In the next few minutes the symmetry of the structure was broken up by wind currents at various altitudes so the shape of the cloud cannot be described in any geometrical manner. In about 8 minutes the top of the cloud was at approximately 40,000 feet as close as I could estimate from our altitude of 24,000 feet and this seemed to be the maximum altitude attained by the cloud. I did not feel the shock wave hit the plane but the pilot felt the reaction on the rudder through the rudder pedals. Some of the other passengers in the plane noted a rather small shock at the time but it was not apparent to me.

KENNETH GREISEN, 1918–2007

Kenneth Ingvard Greisen was an American physicist who worked on nuclear physics and the astrophysics of cosmic rays and gamma radiation. From 1943 to 1946, Greisen was one of the leaders of the detonation team, and he was an observer at the Trinity Test on July 16, 1945.

He was the leader of Group X-1A (photography with flash X-rays) until it was dissolved in May 1945. He then became the leader of the Group X-7 (detonator developments). His wife, Elizabeth, accompanied him to Los Alamos during the war.

After the war, he worked as professor of physics and astronomy at Cornell University. Later in life, he had years of ill health, including a heart attack in 1971, a stroke in 1984 and colon cancer in 1991. He passed away on March 17, 2007, at a hospice care residence in Ithaca, New York.

> *A group of us were lying on the ground just outside of base camp* [ten miles from the charge], *and received time signals over the radio, warning us when the shot would occur. I was personally nervous, for my group had prepared and installed the detonators, and if the shot turned out to be a dud, it might possibly be our fault. We were pretty sure we had done our job well, but there is always some chance of a slip.*
>
> *At minus about 15 seconds I put my head close to the ground, turned to look away from the tower, and put up a shield between my head and the tower. I probably also closed my eyes briefly just before the shot. Suddenly I felt heat on the side of my head toward the tower, opened my eyes and saw a brilliant yellow-white light all around. The heat and light were as though the sun had just come out with unusual brilliance. About a second later I turned to look at the tower through the dark welding glass. A tremendous cloud of smoke was pouring upwards, some parts having brilliant red and yellow colors, like clouds at sunset. These parts kept folding over and over like dough in a mixing bowl. At this time I believe I exclaimed, "My god, it worked!" and felt a great relief.*
>
> *When the intensity of the light had diminished, I put away the glass and looked toward the tower directly. At about this time I noticed a blue color surrounding the smoke cloud. Then someone shouted that we should observe the shock wave travelling along the ground. The appearance of this was a brightly lighted circular area, near the ground, slowly spreading out towards us. The color was yellow.*
>
> *At what I presume was about 50 seconds after the shot, the ground shock and sound reached us almost simultaneously. The noise lasted for a long time, echoing back and forth from the hills. I noticed no sharp crack, but a rumbling sound as of thunder. After the brilliant optical display we had seen, the ground shock and noise were disappointing. No damage occurred, and we were not at all severely shaken.*
>
> *Between the appearance of light and the arrival of the sound, there was loud cheering in the group around us. After the noise was over, we all went about congratulating each other and shaking hands. I believe we were all much more shaken up by the shot mentally than physically.*

The permanence of the smoke cloud was one thing that surprised me. After the first rapid explosion, the lower part of the cloud seemed to assume a fixed shape and to remain hanging motionless in the air. The upper part meanwhile continued to rise, so that after a few minutes it was at least five miles high. It slowly assumed a zigzag shape because of the changing wind velocity at different altitudes. The smoke had pierced a cloud early in its ascent, and seemed to be completely unaffected by the cloud.

EDWIN M. MCMILLAN, 1907–1991

Edwin M. McMillan was an American physicist and Nobel laureate credited with being the first to produce a transuranium element, neptunium. For this, he shared the Nobel Prize in Chemistry with Glenn Seaborg in 1951. In 1953, he became director at the Berkeley Radiation Laboratory and retired from that position in 1973.

Dr. Edwin M. McMillan and Dr. Ernest O. Lawrence working in a lab in Berkeley, California, 1930. *Photo courtesy of the U.S. Department of Energy.*

He died at home in California from complications due to diabetes in 1991.

I shall try to describe the Trinity test as seen from the "Hill Station," 20 miles from the event. None of my estimates of times or magnitudes can be considered very accurate, as I have found by comparison with others a wide variation, illustrating the difficulty of personal judgment without instruments.

The shot went off at about 5:30 a.m., just before sunrise. I was watching the shot through a piece of dark glass such as is used in welders' helmets. An exceedingly bright light appeared and expanded very rapidly. I was aware of a sensation of heat on my face and hands, which lasted about a second. After about two seconds, I took the glass away. The sky and surrounding landscape were brightly illuminated, but not as strongly as in full sunlight. The "ball of fire" was still too bright for direct observation, but it could be seen to be rising and expanding and slowly fading out. At some time during this stage, the layers of clouds visible above the explosion evaporated, forming a hole which rapidly got bigger.

At about 30 seconds, the general appearance was similar to a goblet; the ball I estimated to be about a mile in diameter and about four miles above the ground, glowing with a dull red; a dark stem connected it with the ground, and spread out in a thin dust layer that extended to a radius of about six miles. When the red glow faded out a most remarkable effect made its appearance. The whole surface of the ball was covered with a purple luminescence, like that produced by the electrical excitation of air, and caused undoubtedly by the radioactivity of the material in the ball. This was visible for about five seconds; by this time the sunlight was becoming bright enough to obscure luminous effects.

At some time near the end of the luminescence (I am not sure whether it was before or after) a great cloud broke out of the top of the ball and rose very rapidly to a height of about eight miles, expanding to a rather irregular shape several times as large as the ball. At about two minutes, the blast came. It was remarkably sharp, being more of a "crack" than a "boom." I did not feel any earth shock.

The later stages of motion of the cloud consisted of a slow drifting in the wind, showing the existence of several different wind directions at different altitudes. A current at a few hundred feet carrying the lower part of the "stem" toward the North 10,000 station was particularly striking. The cloud was a different color than the ordinary clouds through which it passed, having a brownish tinge; this could be caused by nitrogen dioxide formed from air by the intense ionization.

The whole spectacle was so tremendous, and one might almost say fantastic that the immediate reaction of the watchers was one of awe rather than excitement. After some minutes of silence, a few people made remarks like, "Well, it worked," and then conversation and discussion became general. I am sure that all who witnessed this test went away with a profound feeling that they had seen one of the great events of history.

Philip Morrison, 1915–2005

Philip Morrison was a professor of physics at the Massachusetts Institute of Technology (MIT). In addition to his work on the Manhattan Project during World War II, he is known for his later work in quantum physics, nuclear physics and high-energy astrophysics.

After the war, he became a champion of nuclear nonproliferation, writing for the *Bulletin of the Atomic Scientists*, and helped found the Federation of American Scientists and the Institute for Defense and Disarmament Studies.

He published papers on cosmic rays, and a 1958 paper of his is considered to mark the birth of gamma ray astronomy. He was known for his articles, books and television programs, producing sixty-eight popular science articles between 1949 and 1976, ten of which were in issues of *Scientific American*.

Morrison died of a respiratory failure in his sleep at his home in Cambridge, Massachusetts, on April 22, 2005.

I observed the Trinity shot looking toward Zero from a position on the south bank of the base camp reservoir directly beside the larger water tank. There were three distinct stages in the process I saw, which I describe consecutively as follows:

1. Instantaneous glow and ball of fire

At time T=-45 seconds I lay prone facing Zero wearing ordinary sun glasses and holding in one hand a stop watch and in the other the welding glass issued by the stockroom. I watched the second-hand until T=-5 seconds when I lowered my head onto the sand bank in such a way that a slight rise in the ground completely shielded me from Zero. I placed the welding glass over the right lens of my sun glasses, the left lens of which was covered by an opaque cardboard shield. I counted seconds and at zero began to raise my head just over the protecting rise. During this motion the gadget went off while I was looking at it or possibly a small fraction of a second before. What I saw first was a brilliant violet glow entering my eyes by reflection from the ground and from the surroundings generally. I had not raised my head quite enough to provide a clear vision of Zero. Immediately after this brilliant violet flash, which was somewhat blinding, I observed through the welding glass, centered at the direction of the tower an enormous and brilliant disk of white light. The sensation lasted for such a short time and the light was so great that I cannot be sure of the shape observed. I remember it only as a well-marked vaguely round pattern. This disk was a true white in color, even through the welding glass which makes the sun's disk distinctly deep green. On subsequently looking at the noon sun through these glasses I have been led to estimate this initial stage of the gadget as corresponding to a color much whiter or bluer and a brightness several times greater than that of the noon sun. I felt a strong sensation of heat on the exposed skin of face and arms, lasting for several seconds and at least as intense as the direct noon sun.

It should be noted that my eyes were adapted to twilight or perhaps even to somewhat brighter light because of the use of the radio dial light I had made just previous to the T -45 second signal.

2. Growth of the mushroom

For a time which I guess to be less than two seconds the bright disk produced an after effect in my eyes which spoiled the details of the following process. I quickly realized that my vision was improving, that the image was becoming much fainter and less white. I then took off the welding glass and several seconds later the sun glasses as well. Beginning at T=+2 to 3 seconds, I observed the somewhat yellowed disk beginning to be eaten into from below by dark obscuring matter. Meanwhile the whole surface of the plain was covered with matter being thrown up into the air as the motion continued outward from Zero. In a matter of a few seconds more the disk had nearly stopped growing horizontally and was beginning to extend in a vertical direction while its appearance had transformed into that of a bright glowing distinctly red column of flame mixed with swirling obscuring matter. The column looked rather like smoke and flame rising from an oil fire. This turbulent red column rose straight up several thousand feet in a few seconds growing a mushroom-like head of the same kind. This mushroom was fully developed and the whole glowing structure complete at about 15,000 feet altitude. I do not recall whether this stage was reached before or after the arrival of the shock. At T +30 I realized the shock was due very soon and I huddled closer to the ground in anticipation of a severe shock. The arrival of the air shock at T +45 on my stop-watch came as an anti-climax. I noticed two deep thuds which sounded rather like a kettle drum rhythm being played some distance away. I remember the sound as being without any important high frequency components as cracks, etc. There was no earth tremor perceptible to me at any time. The ground on which I was lying was a very loosely packed dike of mud.

3. Appearance of the smoke cloud

After the passage of the shock I stood up to watch the end of the mushroom. The red glow died out and the mushroom appeared as a column of smoke or cloud hanging over Zero. In a matter of another minute or so the smoke had arranged itself in three rather well defined oblique clouds forming roughly a vertical Z. The lowest cloud was quite well defined, and stretched north at a slight angle. At a couple of thousand feet, it appeared to bend around almost double and to stretch about southeast for a somewhat greater distance. This second cloud again seemed broken off rather sharply and a large cloud gradually spread with less and less well defined shape from the upper end of the second step. This process was nearly complete when the upper cap was spread over most of the bowl at a height of about 30,000 feet. There was a strong impression of definite layers in the wind structure, and there were even some water vapor clouds which seemed to mark the boundaries between winds of different directions. The completion of this stage took many minutes until finally the cloud was rather well dispersed toward north 10,000 at a rather low level, had overspread at an intermediate level all the way to the Oscuro Mountains, and on a higher level was drifting slowly south and southeast.

Other observations:

After T=+50 seconds, I distinctly smelled upon standing up a faint but marked odor of ozone or corona discharge ionization.

At T +15 minutes or more I observed Zero through a battery commander's periscope set of 8-power. Not much detail was visible in this region. A sort of dust haze seemed to cover the area. A remarkable amount of heat shimmer was noticed on the horizon directly above the Zero area. It was shortly after this that I saw the Jumbo tower was missing.

Size and distance figures mentioned here are based on judgments of angular size and the assumption of 18,000 yards distance from Zero to base camp.

Robert Serber, 1909–1997

Robert Serber was an American physicist. He moved to Los Alamos in 1943, and his five lectures explaining the basic principles and goals of the project were printed and supplied to all incoming scientific staff and became known as the Los Alamos Primer. The *New York Times* labeled him as "the intellectual midwife at the birth of the atomic bomb."

Serber was supposed to go on the camera plane for the Nagasaki mission but was ordered off because he had forgotten his parachute. He was with the first American team to enter Hiroshima and Nagasaki to assess the results of the atomic bombing of the two cities.

He died in 1997 of complications from surgery for brain cancer at his home in Manhattan.

> *I viewed the test, with the Coordinating Committee expedition, from a point about 20 miles away. At the instant of the explosion I was looking directly at it, with no eye protection of any kind. I saw first a yellow glow, which grew almost instantly into an overwhelming white flash, so intense that I was completely blinded. There was a definite sensation of heat. The brilliant illumination seemed to last for about three to five seconds, changing to yellow and then to red; at this stage it appeared to have a radius of about twenty degrees. The first thing I succeeded in seeing after being blinded by the flash looked like a dark violet column several thousand feet high. This column must actually have been quite bright, or I would not have been able to distinguish it. By twenty or thirty seconds after the explosion I was regaining normal vision. At a height of perhaps twenty thousand feet, two or three thin horizontal layers of shimmering white cloud were formed, perhaps due to condensation in the negative phase of the shock wave. Some time later, the noise of the explosion reached us. It had the quality of distant thunder, but was louder. The sound, due to reflections from nearby hills, returned and repeated and reverberated for several seconds, very much like thunder. A column of white smoke appeared over the point of the explosion, rising very rapidly, and spreading slightly as it rose. In a few seconds it reached cloud level, and the clouds in the immediate neighborhood seemed to evaporate and disappear. The column continued to rise and spread to a height of about twice the cloud level. There was no appearance of mushrooming at any height. A smoke cloud also was spreading near ground level.*
>
> *The grandeur and magnitude of the phenomenon were completely breath-taking.*

MAURICE M. SHAPIRO, 1915–2008

Maurice Shapiro studied underwater explosions at Los Alamos during the Manhattan Project. He was the head of a water effects group in the ordnance division and a consultant on hydrodynamics. He served to calculate ballistics tables used in the Hiroshima and Nagasaki bombing missions.

A researcher in the field of cosmic rays and neutrino astrophysics, Shapiro died in Virginia in 2008 at the age of ninety-two.

> *During the Trinity test, I was stationed about 20 miles away, with the members of the Coordinating Council.*
>
> *At the time of the initial flash of light my eyes were not protected, and I was momentarily blinded, much as one would be in emerging suddenly from a dark room into bright sunlight. After a couple of seconds I regained sufficient sight to see the entire sky (in the direction of Trinity) aglow with an orange hue. This glow disappeared after a second or two, and then I saw a column of dark gases rising toward the overhanging clouds. Several people near me commented on the violet color of the cloud of gas, but I observed no such color, presumably because of the initial effect on my eyes. I estimated the width (or diameter) of the column of gas as roughly 1/5 mile. After a few minutes this column rose to a height which I judged to be 8 or 10 miles high, and then it spread laterally. There were a few small puffs of white vapor, which I interpreted as arising from a "cloud-chamber effect" (supersaturation followed by condensation of moisture).*
>
> *The shock wave from the explosion arrived at about one and a half minutes after the flash of light, and I heard it as a sharp report. Although I had expected it, the intensity of the blast startled me. My impression at the time was that an enemy observer stationed about 20 miles from the scene of delivery would be deeply impressed, to say the least.*

CYRIL S. SMITH, 1903–1992

Cyril Stanley Smith was a British science historian and metallurgist. For the Manhattan Project, he was responsible for the production of fissionable metals working with uranium-235 and plutonium. After the war, Smith founded the Institute for the Study of Metals at the University of Chicago.

Since this [the Trinity shot] *took place over a week ago my impressions have undoubtedly been modified very considerably by subsequent discussion and many features have faded from memory.*

I was located at the base camp, behind a five foot embankment near the water tanks at T=0. I was facing away from the shot, somewhat bent down below the top of the bank. In addition, my eyes were partly covered by a welder's glass. For a time estimated as two seconds (though it may have been less) I was watching the ground through the corner of my eye. Even though this was lighted by reflection from the clouds, it was intensely bright and apparently free from color. Since the shot there has been some discussion of the duration of this intense light, but it is definitely my recollection that I opened and closed my eyes several times and waited for the light to decrease in intensity before turning to face the reaction zone directly. Even after the estimated 2 seconds the light was still intense enough to be clearly seen through the welder's glass but there was no direct ball of fire or structure or any symmetry, this part of the phenomenon evidently having ceased.

The appearance of a turbulent gas apparently undergoing combustion was quite surprising. It looked not much different from the film of the 100 ton shot or any large fire, for instance an oil tank fire or the Graf Zeppelin. After another second or two I removed the welder's glass and looked directly. As the main light became less intense, the bluish ionization zone became visible, extending to a diameter almost twice that of the area where there was incandescence. I noticed a dust cloud travelling near the ground, and at some stage (I am not sure whether early or late in the proceedings, but it was definitely illuminated by the shot) I noticed a ring, supposedly of moisture condensed by the rarefaction wave, at a level slightly below the clouds. This ring did not spread, but once formed seemed to remain stationary.

The instant after the shot, my reactions were compounded of relief that "it worked"; consciousness of extreme silence, and a momentary question as to whether we had done more than we intended. Practically none of the watchers made any vocal comment until after the shock wave had passed and even then the cheers were not intense or prolonged. The elation of most observers seemed to increase for a period of 30 minutes afterwards, as they had a chance to absorb the significance of the achievement.

The rising of the cloud of reaction products to above the cloud level seems to have proceeded rapidly but in a normal fashion. It was noticeable that there were a number of rough projections, indicating high local turbulence. Shortly after the smoke column with its mushroom top was formed, wind currents distorted it into a jagged or corkscrew appearance. There was a dust cloud over the ground, extending for a considerable distance. A cloud, whether of dust or moisture particles, hung close to the ground and slowly drifted east into the hills, persisting for over an hour.

The obvious fact that all of the reaction products were not proceeding upward in a neat ball but were lagging behind and being blown by low altitude winds over the ground in the direction of inhabited areas produced very definite reflection that this is not a pleasant weapon we have produced. Later reflections were on the manner of defense against it and the realization that a city is henceforth not the place in which to live.

I repeat that no attention should be paid to any comment made in this report, since the described events occurred many days ago.

Victor F. Weisskopf, 1908–2002

Victor Frederick Weisskopf was a theoretical physicist who served as the leader of the theoretical division of the Manhattan Project. Later, he was a cofounder and board member of the Union of Concerned Scientists and campaigned against the proliferation of nuclear weapons.

In a lecture at MIT in 1991, he said the rationale for dropping the bomb on Hiroshima in 1945 was for the destruction to have a strong psychological effect on Japan. The second bomb, dropped on Nagasaki three days later, was more troubling to him.

"The second bomb I don't hesitate to call a crime," Weisskopf told the audience at the 1991 lecture.

After the war, he joined the faculty at the Massachusetts Institute of Technology and ultimately became head of the department. He was known as an inspirational teacher, encouraging students to ask questions and think like physicists—not just to learn physics. He died at ninety-three at home in Massachusetts.

I was located at base camp and watched the phenomenon from a little ridge about 100 yds. east of the water tower. Groups of observers had arranged small wooden sticks at a distance of 10 yards from our observation place in order to estimate the size of the explosion. They were arranged so that their distance corresponded to 1000-feet at zero point. I looked at the explosion through the dark glass, but I have provided for an indirect view of the landscape in order to see the deflected light.

When the explosion went off, I was first dazzled by this indirect light which was much stronger than I anticipated, and I was not able to concentrate upon the view through the dark glass and missed, therefore, the first stages of the explosion. When I was able to look through the dark glass I saw flames and smoke of an estimated diameter of 1,000 yards. which was slowly decreasing in brightness seemingly due to more smoke development. At the same time it rose slightly above the surface. After about three seconds its intensity was so low I could remove the dark glass and look at it directly. Then I saw a reddish glowing smoke ball rising with a thick stem of dark brown color. This smoke ball was surrounded by a blue glow which clearly indicated a strong radioactivity and was certainly due to the gamma rays emitted by the cloud into the surrounding air. At that moment the cloud had about 1,000 billions of curies of radioactivity whose radiation must have produced the blue glow.

The first two or three seconds, I felt very strongly the heat radiation all over the exposed parts of my body. The part of my retina which was exposed to the indirect light from the surrounding mountains was completely blinded and I could feel traces of the after image 30 minutes after the shock.

The reddish cloud darkened after about 10 or 20 seconds and rose rather rapidly leaving behind a thick stem of dark brown smoke. After this, I remember having seen a white hemisphere rising above the clouds in continuation of the breakthrough of the explosion cloud through the ordinary cloud level.

The path of the shock wave through the clouds was plainly visible as an expanding circle all over the sky where it was covered by clouds. After about 45 seconds the sound wave arrived, and it struck me as being much weaker than anticipated.

"A few people laughed, a few people cried, most people were silent," Oppenheimer has said about the experience in that S-10,000 bunker. "There floated through my mind a line from the Bhagavad-Gita in which Krishna is trying to persuade the Prince that he should do his duty: 'I am become death, the shatterer of worlds.'"

"People congratulated him as he came out of the bunker to view the mighty rising fireball for the first time," Peter Goodchild wrote in his book *J. Robert Oppenheimer: Shatterer of Worlds*. "There he [Oppenheimer] met up with the frenziedly-excited [George] Kistiakowsky." Earlier in July, Oppenheimer had bet Kistiakowsky ten dollars against the explosive expert's whole salary that the gadget wouldn't work.

Left: Kenneth Bainbridge served as Trinity Test director. *Photo courtesy Los Alamos National Laboratories.*

Below: Ken Bainbridge (*left*) and Robert Wilson toast each other with cups of ice water after being interviewed by the Smithsonian at Ground Zero in 1988. Behind them is the Dave McDonald ranch house at base camp. The two men were important to the success of the test at Trinity and worked hard after the war to make sure nuclear weapons were under civilian control and were never used again. *Photo courtesy of White Sands Missile Range.*

"I remember making a rather silly remark," Kistiakowsky said. "I suppose it was because of the tension of the last forty-eight hours.…I slapped him on the back and I said, 'Oppie, I won the bet.' In reply Oppenheimer, who was obviously at the height of emotional tension, couldn't do anything but pull out his bill folder and then he turned to round and said, 'George, I don't have it.'"

Shortly after this, Ken Bainbridge, solid, dependable, flushed with the success of his test, came up to Oppenheimer and grasped his hand. "Oppie," he said, "now we're all sons of bitches."

4

INTO A NEW WORLD

William L. Laurence was recruited away from the *New York Times* at the request of General Groves to be a War Department historian for the army. As such, he was asked to write several versions of the press release following the Trinity explosion, describing it as an ammunition dump explosion. He was on-site as the only journalist allowed at the explosion and later wrote several accounts of it. He was also present for the bombing of Nagasaki, ultimately earned two Pulitzer Prizes and is credited for coining the term the "atomic age."

In his book, Laurence recounts:

> *The Atomic Age began at exactly 5:30 mountain war time on the morning of July 16, 1945, on a stretch of semidesert land about 50 airline miles from Alamagordo,* [sic] *N.M., just a few minutes before the dawn of a new day on this earth.*
>
> *At that great moment in history, ranking with the moment in the long ago when man first put fire to work for him and started on his march to civilization, the vast energy locked within the hearts of the atoms of matter was released for the first time in a burst of flame such as had never before been seen on this planet, illuminating earth and sky for a brief span that seemed eternal with the light of many supersuns.*
>
> *The elemental flame, the first fire ever made on earth that did not have its origin in the sun, came from the explosion of the atomic bomb. It was a full-dress rehearsal preparatory to use the bomb over Hiroshima and Nagaski. . . .*

It was a sunrise such as the world had never seen, a great green supersun climbing in a fraction of a second to a height of more than 8,000 feet, rising ever higher until it touched the clouds, lighting up earth and sky all around with a dazzling luminosity.

Up it went, a great ball of fire about a mile in diameter, changing colors as it kept shooting upward, from deep purple to orange, expanding, growing bigger, rising as it was expanding, an elemental force freed from its bonds after being chained for billions of years.

For a fleeting instant the color was unearthly green, such as one sees only in the corona of the sun during a total eclipse.

It was as though the earth had opened and the skies had split. One felt as though he had been privileged to witness the Birth of the World—to be present at the moment of Creation when the Lord said: Let There be Light.

Berlyn Brixner, photographer from El Paso, was the regional photographer for the soil conservation office in Albuquerque when a friend told him about a job with the United States Engineers in Santa Fe. He worked with a high-speed camera manufactured at Los Alamos to photograph the implosion process of the bomb.

Brixner's objective as the head photographer for the Manhattan Project was to photograph all aspects of an unknown and unpredictable event that began with the brightest flash of light ever produced on Earth. To accomplish this, Brixner incorporated fifty cameras of various running speeds, using sixteen-millimeter black-and-white film positioned at different locations to capture in full and slow motion. These cameras were positioned at every possible angle, distance and film speed. All of the cameras, including the one he had in his lap at the time of the atomic bomb's detonation, were operated from a central control station. Approximately 100,000 photographs were made of the Trinity atomic bomb test.

Brixner talked with the *El Paso Times* for a July 17, 1983 story. He said the actual test detonation of the atomic bomb was "unbelievable, really." Brixner was huddled with most of his cameras in one of the earth-and-concrete-reinforced observation shelters. This one was ten thousand yards north of the tower—as close as anyone. The observers had been issued aluminum face shields with welder's goggles for viewing windows. At detonation, Brixner's shield seemed to light up like the sun. He turned away and caught sight of the Oscura Mountains bathed in radiance. He scanned them for a few seconds and then looked through the shield again.

White Sands Missile Range public information officer Jim Eckles interviewed Berlyn Brixner at the April 7, 1990 Trinity Site open house. *Photo courtesy of White Sands Missile Range.*

One of the very first images recorded as the first atomic bomb explodes in the New Mexico desert. This is one of approximately 100,000 photographs made of the test by Berlyn Brixner and his fifty cameras around the site. "It looked like a giant magnesium flare which kept on for what seemed like a whole minute but was actually one or two seconds," said Hans Bethe. *Photo courtesy of White Sands Missile Range.*

He saw a ball of fire rising, and he panned a motion picture camera to follow the fire ball. It rose forty-one thousand feet, as tall as Mount Everest, and the shock wave hit about twenty seconds later.

When the fire went out, a dust cloud remained, surrounded by a blue haze of radioactivity. This cloud, moving northwest, dissipated around dawn. While Brixner was busy unloading his cameras, a medical doctor in charge of monitoring radiation at the shelter, Henry Barnett, gave orders to evacuate the bunker. Brixner simply declined. He insisted on making sure his film was unloaded and stowed in a truck. He was scared. A red haze was descending from the clouds. Bixner tossed the last of his film into the truck and jumped in himself. The truck took off.

It later proved to be a false alarm. Film badges worn by the personnel at the observation point indicated that no radioactivity had reached the shelter.

The clouds had drifted northeast at ten miles per hour, showering potentially radioactive ash on Carrizozo about forty miles east and dropping some residual and possibly radioactive ash on northern communities, Coyote, Ancho, Ecolote and Vaughn. The army had stationed men as far away as one hundred miles to evacuate towns and ranches if radioactivity proved a threat.

Brixner had set one camera eight hundred yards from the tower. A lead-lined tank that went into the area immediately after the explosion to record the devastation pulled the camera out on a long drag cable. The tank was driven by Sergeant Bill Smith and was carrying Herbert Anderson and Enrico Fermi. It moved into Ground Zero to recover equipment and study debris in hopes of getting information on long-range detection of atomic explosions. The tank was equipped with a trapdoor through which earth samples could be safely picked up in the crater.

Anderson reported his first view of the crater. He saw what looked like a great jade blossom amid the coppery sands of the desert. Where the shot tower had stood was a crater of glittering green glass. The fireball had sucked up the dirt, fused it and dumped the particles back on the explosion point. They lay there inside a 1,200-foot-wide saucer, 25 feet deep at the center. The tower's concrete stumps, which once stood above ground, had been crushed to a depth of seven feet beneath the sand.

Three months later, after radioactivity had cooled, Brixner walked over Ground Zero at Trinity Site. Heat had fused the desert sand into glass, stained green by the melted iron tower.

Brixner photographed the trinitite and walked on it and thought about the birth of the nuclear age, which he had recorded on film. He continued

J. Robert Oppenheimer and General Leslie Groves survey the remnants of the testing tower at Ground Zero on the Trinity Test site in September 1945. *Photo courtesy of the U.S. Department of Energy.*

to work at Los Alamos National Laboratory, which became a research center for solar and fusion energy and weapons, until he retired in 1978.

Jack Aeby was one of the first civilian employees on the Manhattan Project. He described himself as a jack-of-all-trades for the health physics group. He had nothing to do on the morning of the Trinity Test, so his boss, Emilio Segre, got him approved to be at the site with a camera. Aeby's photo of the test is the only known color image of the explosion.

He recalled:

> *I finagled a roll of—not Kodachrome, oh it was the German photo outfit, a 100-foot length of color film, which offloaded into a cartridge or several cartridges, and carried it at Trinity. Film was hard to come by during the war, certainly color film, so that worked fine. By the time I got around to the actual test itself I only had 4 exposures left on the film I had taken down there, so I had to hoard it very carefully, and that was a serious error because that was the most interesting part.*
>
> *But the night of the detonation I moved out away from the area in which we were sitting and out to where the lights of the community area were in front of me, used—turned a chair backwards and I'd carry it out there and sat in it using that as a tripod, aimed the camera at the detonation point, which was roughly 6,000 yards away. I don't know how many miles that was, about three I think. At any rate, I opened the shutter all the way as it was not clear we were going to get any kind of yield or detonation out of this experimental device—that's what it was, it wasn't a bomb or any such, it was a chunk of material surrounded by high explosives.*
>
> *Well anyhow, I opened the shutter wide—the full way, full stop—and put the shutter on bulb and held it open. It was black out, just ahead of the detonation, and when it went off it became clear that it was a good yield. I released the shutter, it closed, I cranked the exposure down to where it was reasonable, about 1,000 per second, and fired the other three shots in rapid succession. The middle one, by luck, turned out to be just about the right exposure—the other two were useable but not as clear or in focus, all this good stuff.*

In February 1984, the *Albuquerque Journal* ran a story about an air force flight engineer who was in the area of the Trinity Test and was not supposed to be. Howard McNeil was stationed at Roswell and was part of the crew of a new B-29 bomber that took off on a training flight. Curious about

Jack Aeby during a return visit to Trinity Site in 2005. *Photo courtesy of White Sands Missile Range.*

an impossible sunrise in the west—probably an ammunition dump explosion, they thought—he and five others unwittingly piloted themselves over the test site within an hour of the blast.

"It wasn't until weeks later that I realized I had flown through a damn radioactive cloud," McNeil told reporter Leah Beth Ward.

McNeil was an enlisted man at the time of the Trinity Test. He was twenty-four years old and was wondering if he was going to be sent to Guam like a lot of the other B-29 crews at Roswell.

"The group there [at Roswell] was called something like the Silver Plate Bomb Squadron. These were the guys that would go to Guam with the bomb, even though most of them didn't have any idea they were carrying them. These guys would kid us and say, 'Hey you're just goofing off here.' It wasn't until much later that the guilt [associated with using the bomb] hit a lot of people."

A navigational map the crews had did outline certain restricted areas in red. McNeil said those areas were generally thought to be munitions sites. So, that is what they thought about Trinity Site when they saw the "sunrise."

"We were getting ready to take off, and all the sudden the sun came up out of the west. We said they must have blown up a big one this time and took off to find it. We didn't see the mushroom, but we saw layers upon layers of clouds forming in the sky, one on top of the other. The colors started out orange and then over the next two or three minutes became purple. It was such an awesome thing, you don't realize how much time has gone by, whether it's a few seconds or minutes."

McNeil said he dropped altitude from about twenty-two thousand to ten thousand feet to see the "fire." They were looking for trucks scurrying around in the aftermath of an ammunition explosion but saw none. "We thought we'd see a great big hole, or bunkers or something. The co-pilot did see a shiny spot in the middle of the desert. We didn't know what was going on, so we just kind of gave up and went back."

After the atomic bomb was dropped from a B-29 on Hiroshima on August 6, 1945, he understood the nature of the mysterious explosion, but McNeil said he didn't begin to think about his probable exposure to radiation until the government—in the 1950s—began issuing warnings to people near the Nevada test site.

"When I heard about this thing in Hiroshima, I thought, 'Hey, that might be the same thing.' Hell, they didn't tell enlisted men anything. As time went on, we heard more and more about radiation. There's a lot of guinea pigs in this world. My feeling was that I shouldn't have been flying around in that area, so I didn't tell anybody what happened. To do so now would be an exercise in futility."

Looking back forty years from the time of the *Journal* interview, McNeil recognized his unique vantage point on history that day and the destructive force it represented. He said it made him more philosophical.

"I saw the beginning of the atomic age. There's not many things that happen like that in anyone's life. But what happens to a lot of people in the military—especially the Air Force—is that you're dropping bombs, you're up there in the sky and you can't see the people you're hitting. The thing we all hope is that for our grandchildren's sake, if we've got people smart

Oppenheimer and Groves (*center*), surrounded by officials and reporters, examine one of the tower footings on the crater floor. *Photo courtesy of New Mexico State University Library, Archives and Special Collections.*

enough to make these kinds of weapons, we're smart enough to find a way not to use them. It's so stupid."

In the meantime, in Carrizozo, Alvin and Elizabeth Graves were set up at Harry Miller's Tourist Court the day before the test with a seismograph, Geiger counter, short-wave radio and portable electric generator. At 3:00 p.m. after the Trinity test, the Graveses began getting disturbing readings on their Geiger counter, and at 4:20 p.m., the counter shot off scale, and Alvin called base camp. The fate of the people of Carrizozo hung in the balance while the scientists and military decided whether to evacuate it. They held off, and the radioactive cloud passed over within hours, and the readings dropped.

5
IN THE DISTANCE

Outside of the immediate communities of Otero, Socorro and Lincoln Counties, others experienced the Trinity Site explosion in their own areas. Across mountains and deserts, people felt, heard or saw effects. The flash of light was reportedly seen in Albuquerque, Santa Fe, Silver City, Gallup and El Paso. Windows rattled in Silver City and Gallup.

Terry Humbolt's father was a miner in the mines near Silver City, and Terry later heard his grandparents talking about it. "We lived right next to the open pit, so we were always feeling the blast," Humbolt said. "You wouldn't even think about it when you felt the earth move. Evidently, that was a shaker, and anybody who was out working in the mine could kind of see it light up a little bit. Then word got out it was a government ammunition dump."

A bright flash of light and high winds marking the detonations of the Trinity Test were observed at the headquarters of the Jornada Experimental Station, according to Roy Stovall in a 2012 interview with the New Mexico Farm and Ranch Heritage Museum Oral History Project. The station is west of the San Andres Mountains near the city of Las Cruces.

"I had gone out that morning, had a porch all around the house," Stovall said. "I just left the bedroom and saw this light flash, and I thought somebody had turned the lights on, the switch. And [*sic*] but it wasn't. It was a big flash in the sky, and then a real hard windstorm come right after that. Nobody knew what went off, you know." (Interviewer Donna Wojcik said the San Andreas separated the Experimental Station from Trinity Site.

Wojcik also said during the interview that when the museum was working on a POW in Agriculture exhibit, some of the people they interviewed who had been stationed in Lordsburg at the time had said they saw the light "away over in Lordsburg."

Santa Fe Railroad engineer Ed Lane's train was zooming through Belen en route to El Paso when he saw what he thought was either a severe electrical storm in the Sandia Mountains or a fiery meteor. By the time he reached El Paso, he had decided to tell his story to the local papers. The *El Paso Herald-Post*'s city editor thought Lane had an experienced an optical illusion, but calls from other correspondents, plus corroborating reports from the Associated Press, convinced the editor to replat the front page for the afternoon edition.

In El Paso itself, 130 miles due south of Trinity Site, people thought the horizon was on fire. It was one of those muggy mornings, Jack Coulehan of El Paso told Pat Henry in a July 17, 1983 *El Paso Time*s story. The sky was cloudy but not completely overcast that day. Coulehan and two other printers were riding south on Alabama Street to their 6:00 a.m. shift at Newspaper Printing Corporation.

"We were still sleepy," Coulehan told Henry. "Suddenly, lightning lit up the clouds. But it lasted longer than lightning. We stopped the car and looked around. We thought a plane had crashed."

While working on that afternoon's edition, they read that an ammunition dump had exploded at Alamogordo. That satisfied Coulehan. After A-bombs were dropped on Hiroshima and Nagasaki, Japan, the real story came out. Coulehan realized he had witnessed the dawning of the nuclear age.

Kay Harper and her husband, Bob, a technical photographer, moved to Los Alamos after the test. But Kay remembers a friend, motor pool driver Elsie Pierce, who claimed to have seen the test from the area. "I had a friend who lived in the mountains there," Kay said. "She knew when they were going to set off the test, and she was looking in that direction, and she saw the lights from the explosion. She was standing on her porch overlooking Omega Canyon southeast right toward where the bomb was supposed to go off."

After hearing it from several fellow residents of Los Alamos, Kay added, "The hundreds of men who worked on it had a doubt about how it would work. Some of them doubted the predictions and were afraid that this kind of explosion, which had never been detonated in our entire solar system, and beyond the fear of these few scientists was that the explosion would be so tremendous, gigantic, unbelievable that it would detonate the atmosphere surrounding the earth, and that would be the end of the earth, it was that or nothing because it was designed to win the war, and it did."

A sleepless patient in the Los Alamos hospital reported seeing a strange light. His wife, waiting on Sawyer's Hill behind Los Alamos, wrote, "Then it came. The blinding light like no other light one had ever seen. The trees, illuminated leaping out. The mountains flashing into life. Later the long slow rumble. Something had happened, all right, for good or ill."

Altus Boulden, born 1928, was out feeding the chickens at his home near Hope, New Mexico, almost two hundred miles east of Trinity Site, when he saw light in the west:

> *I looked over to the west—it's bright over there, it kept getting brighter. It was getting real bright. I went back in the house and called Mother. I said, "Mother, Mother!"*
>
> [She said,] *"What?"*
>
> *I said, "The sun is coming up in the west."*
>
> *She didn't believe me and said, "Do your chores, you've got to go catch that bus, go take your physical." She'd signed the papers at 17 for me to get in.*
>
> *I said, "Mother, it's coming up in the west!" I went back out there and I said, "Come look and see."*
>
> *And I'll never forget that. She walked out at the east and she looked back in the west and said, "Oh my God!" went back in the house and never said another word.*

Altus's wife, Ann Boulden (McElroy), born in 1935, said she was also living in Hope at the time. She recalled:

> *And at this time, it was all dark, Daddy was outside doing chores and things, Mom and I were in the house, and Daddy calls us out. And we go out and we look and, mind you, we're on the one side of the Sacramento Mountains, and Alamogordo is on the other side* [there are two mountain ranges between Hope and the Trinity Site] *and we're twenty-one miles from Artesia, and he calls us out, and we see this big, old semicircle of light on the horizon there over towards Alamogordo. At the time, we didn't know what it was. But it was bright white to start with and then faded gradually to pink. And later on, of course, we heard that it was an explosion, but we didn't hear anything about the "A" bomb until later on.*

Warren Harding Gillie was stationed at the Fort Bayard commissary, about 160 miles southwest of Trinity Site. Of the test, he said:

> *In my office in the hospital at Fort Bayard they had those windows that had weights on each side. When you raised the window, the weights come down. And every window in that hospital shook. And, sound waves bounce, and I guess we hit one of the sound waves because we were quite a ways from there. But we didn't see the mushroom cloud. We didn't hear the noise. But we did get the repercussion from the sound waves. And every window in that hospital shook when I went down from my upstairs residence. I went down to the mess hall, and everybody asked me what that was. I said, "I have no idea. No idea whatsoever."*
>
> *I went out to Trinity Site afterward. And the sand was fused together like glass. It was very interesting. Not green, sand looking. At that time, they never fenced it over like they do today. I was out there prior to all the fence put up or anything like that. And it was quite interesting.*

Gillie said he picked up trinitite from the ground at the site but later gave it to a niece who was in high school to show her class, and she never gave it back.

6

IMMEDIATE EFFECTS

Although what happened at the Trinity Site was not in fact released to the public as anything but "a munitions dump explosion" in a press release, many immediately knew something more must have happened.

The commanding officer at the Alamogordo Army Air Base (now Holloman Air Force Base) issued a statement on July 16, stating, "Several inquiries have been received concerning a heavy explosion which occurred on the Alamogordo Base reservation this morning. A remotely located ammunition magazine containing a considerable amount of high explosives and pyrotechnics exploded. There was no loss of life or injury to anyone, and the property damage outside of the explosives magazine itself was negligible. Weather conditions affecting the content of gas shells exploded by the blast may make it desirable for the Army to evacuate temporarily a few civilians from their homes."

On July 19, 1945, the *Alamogordo News* printed the following story, its first news after the explosion:

> TERRIFIC EXPLOSION WEST OF TULAROSA MONDAY MORNING
>
> *F.E. Calkins, who is engaged in mining at the old Courtney Mine four miles south of High Rolls was awakened by a bright light which lit up his room about 5:30 Monday morning. He sprang out and saw what he thought might be a large airplane explosion west of Tularosa 45 miles away. The light held for several moments before the sound arrived.*
>
> *Reports are that windows rattled at Gallup 235 miles away. Passengers on a train near Mountainair believed a large bomber had exploded.*

SANTA FE NEW MEXICAN

The Oldest Newspaper in the Southwest, Founded in 1849

SANTA FE, NEW MEXICO, MONDAY, AUGUST 6, 1945 — Price 5c

Los Alamos Secret Disclosed by Truman

ATOMIC BOMBS DROP ON JAPAN

Deadliest Weapons in World's History Made In Santa Fe Vicinity

Santa Fe learned officially today of a city of 6,000 in its own front yard.

The reverberating announcement of the Los Alamos bomb, with 2,000 times the power of the great Grand-Slammers dropped on Germany, also lifted the secret of the community on the Pajarito Plateau, whose presence Santa Fe has ignored, except in whispers, for more than two years.

'Utter Destruction,' Promised in Potsdam Ultimatum, Unleashed; Power Equals 2,000 Superforts

WASHINGTON, Aug. 6 (AP)—The U. S. Army Air Force has released on the Japanese an atomic bomb containing more power than 20,000 tons of TNT.

It produces more than 2,000 times the blast of the largest bomb ever used before.

The announcement of the development was made in a statement by President Truman released by the White House today.

The bomb was dropped 16 hours ago on Hiroshima, an important Japanese army base.

The President said that the bomb has "added a new and revolutionary increase in destruction" on the Japanese.

Mr. Truman added:

"It is an atomic bomb. It is a harnessing of the basic power of the universe. The force from which the sun draws its power has been loosed against those who brought war to the Far East."

May Be Tool To End Wars; New Era Seen

4 More Nippon Cities Now Smoldering Ruins

Hi Johnson Dies at 79

Tomato Juice Off Rationing

Now They Can Be Told Aloud, Those Stoories of 'the Hill'

The Weather

New Mexicans were not told what happened at the Trinity Site until after the bombs were dropped on Japan, putting an end to World War II. *Photo courtesy of New Mexico State University Library, Archives and Special Collections.*

> *So brilliant was the flash from the explosion that Miss Georgia Green, former pupil of the New Mexico School for the Blind, being driven to Albuquerque from Socorro by her brother-in-law, exclaimed "What's That?"*
>
> *There has been no enlightenment over the incident from officials at the Alamogordo Air Base.*
>
> *There seemed to be no planes flying in that vicinity at the time, the official report is that there was no loss of life and planes were held at the base for a period after the explosion. So the civilian conjecture is that some experimentation was going on in explosives which required as isolated terrain such as the explosion occurred on.*

OF COWS AND CATS

There are many accounts about animals and the changes in them, mostly cattle, after the explosion, and there are many differing opinions as to what happened to them. In a continuation of the Holm Bursom III account from the previous chapter, he talked about the animals and sheepherders on the Bursom ranch following the Trinity Test:

> *On the ranch itself, we had quite a few cattle that were lying down and asleep at that time, and the side facing the blast—these were Hereford cattle, they were red in color—the side facing the Trinity Site turned white, and several of the sheepherders that were closer, who had black beards—they were all young people—their beards turned white. We had one black cat, in particular, that I know of, that turned white.*
>
> *There were apparently no adverse effects. The Atomic Energy Commission bought two carloads of our livestock and took 'em to Knoxville, Tennessee, and they all died of old age. No adverse effect as far as health or reproduction—they continued to produce normal calves the rest of their producing lives. And none of the sheepherders seemed to have any problem, and I didn't have any problems.*

In a very different account, told to an oral history gatherer with the New Mexico Farm and Ranch Heritage Museum, F. Roe Lovelace, born in 1938, recalled that the government bought up cattle from areas around the bomb site because many of them had white radiation burns on their hides. Trenches were dug, and the cattle were killed and buried in the trenches.

White-faced Herefords on the Pat Withers Ranch in Oscura, New Mexico, in 1952. Animals similar to these were found with altered fur and skin colors following the Trinity Test. *Photo courtesy of Human Systems Research and White Sands Missile Range.*

Lovelace said his father was president of the school board in Corona at the time.

"There was a guy who lived on the Malpais ranch," Lovelace said. "It was so bright. It was like five o'clock in the morning, and it woke him up. He went out to see what that was, you know. The government quietly went around buying all the cattle in the area because the way the cattle were laying down, 'cause it was, you know, before daylight, the side that was up had turned white, so they knew something was wrong. Big wrong."

Lovelace's mother told him about the cows, and she said, "They dug trenches and would kill the cattle and just put them in those trenches and get rid of them, and the government bought all the cattle that year on all around the country."

Phil Harvey Jr., born in 1951, is the grandson of C.M. Harvey, who moved to El Paso in about 1911. The family had ranch land about eighteen miles away from the Trinity Site. Harvey told the New Mexico Farm and Ranch Heritage Museum oral history collector that he remembered hearing stories about how some of their older cattle had white marks on their skin from radiation burn.

"We were talking about Mozaun [one of the ranch workers] driving down from Cloudcroft, goin' to Carrizozo with a load of bulls and seeing a light, and, of course, that was the nuclear explosion at Trinity Site. And he really didn't know what it was but eventually found out," Harvey said. "We had a lot [of cattle]. The ranch was stocked with all Hereford cows, and I remembered the first time, one of the first times, I went up there to the ranch and part of the ranch was called the Mesas on the Chupadera Mesa, not far from Bingham and just north of the Highway 380, and eighteen miles as the crow flies from where the bomb went off. I remember my dad and Mozaun pointing out the cattle—some white marks on 'em. Some of 'em did have white hair. They were older cows."

In the *Alamogordo Daily News* on November 25, 1984, Dr. David Townsend talked about the cows. He confirmed that many of the cattle that had become "mottled," and many Hereford cattle that had their red coloring become "roan."

"They had been grazing in close proximity to Trinity and their strange discoloration appeared soon after the blast and seemed to have resulted from fallout as most of the affected animals were downwind," Townsend wrote. "The U.S. government bought 150 of the cattle, sent 17 of the most seriously affected to Los Alamos, and the remainder to Oak Ridge, Tennessee, for study. The Oak Ridge herd, increased to 211, was turned over to the University of Tennessee."

Townsend came into possession of a copy of a letter from Wright H. Langham, who had been leader of the group dealing with the cattle early on, to Madame Jacqueline Juillard, a Swiss chemist who had inquired about the animals. Langham quoted from the study done by James M. Bird concerning the cattle. Bird compared the exposed cattle to a control herd in his study with some interesting results:

> *The appearance of the hair of the exposed cattle (graying, thin areas, dead-appearing) was an effect of the irradiation. The thin condition of the exposed cattle at the beginning of this study was a nutritional effect rather than from irradiation, based on a comparison of beginning weights, rate of gain and general appearance of both the exposed and control herds. These exposed cattle made satisfactory growth and weight gains when fed an adequate ration. The percent of cattle lost by death was slightly higher in the control herd rather than in the irradiated herd. Pathologic changes in the exposed cattle were most severe in the superficial parts of the skin. There was a marked thickening of the skin, it was non-pliable, firm and fixed with hyperkeratosis. Artificially produced wounds required two to three times as long to heal as similar wounds on control cattle. Less pressure*

Tom McDonald's cattle at the McDonald ranch on the bombing range in a photo taken in the 1930s. *Photo courtesy Howard McDonald.*

was required to incise the skin of exposed animals than the controls. No significant difference was found in the blood picture of the two groups. Both appeared to be within normal range. The calves from exposed cows performed equally as well as the calves from control cows. There was very little difference in the performance of calves by the irradiated sires and control sires. The breeding efficiency and relative fertility were as good in the irradiated herd as in the control herd. Breeding efficiency of all the sires used in this study was satisfactory.

7

THE RANCHERS

The story of the Trinity Site would not be complete without acknowledging the ranchers of the Tularosa Basin, the Jornada del Muerto and the mountain ranges (San Andres and Oscura) that separate those areas. In the late 1800s, many of these ranchers came to New Mexico from Texas looking for land to call their own and vast grasslands to raise their cattle.

The McDonalds—great-grandparents of the McDonald clan who owned three area ranches, including the Schmidt/McDonald house where the bomb was assembled, two miles from Ground Zero, and the base camp ranch house, nine miles from Ground Zero—came from south Texas on a wagon train between 1881 and 1882.

By 1940, homesteads had sprung up across the basin and the hills, where people put their homes and were able to lease the right to use federal and state lands for grazing. In 1942, the government sent those ranching families packing to claim vast swatches of land for military purposes in the face of World War II. The old Alamogordo Bombing Range became a home for rocket experimentation and morphed into White Sands Proving Ground. People were offered compensation for the loss of land but often did not receive the full amount they were promised. Regardless, they lost the homes and lives on the range that they had worked so hard to grow.

In the fall of 1944, when soldiers started arriving at Trinity Site to prepare for the test, base camp was located at the Dave and Ross McDonald ranch about nine miles from the site. The George McDonald ranch house, two miles away, was used as the assembly site for the bomb's plutonium core.

Above: An early chuck wagon from the southern New Mexico ranching life, circa 1918. From left are Tom McDonald and Mack McDonald, brothers who ran their ranches in the area that later became the Trinity Site. *Photo courtesy Howard McDonald.*

Right: Pat Withers at the Robinson place, 1943. *Photo courtesy of Human Systems Research and White Sands Missile Range.*

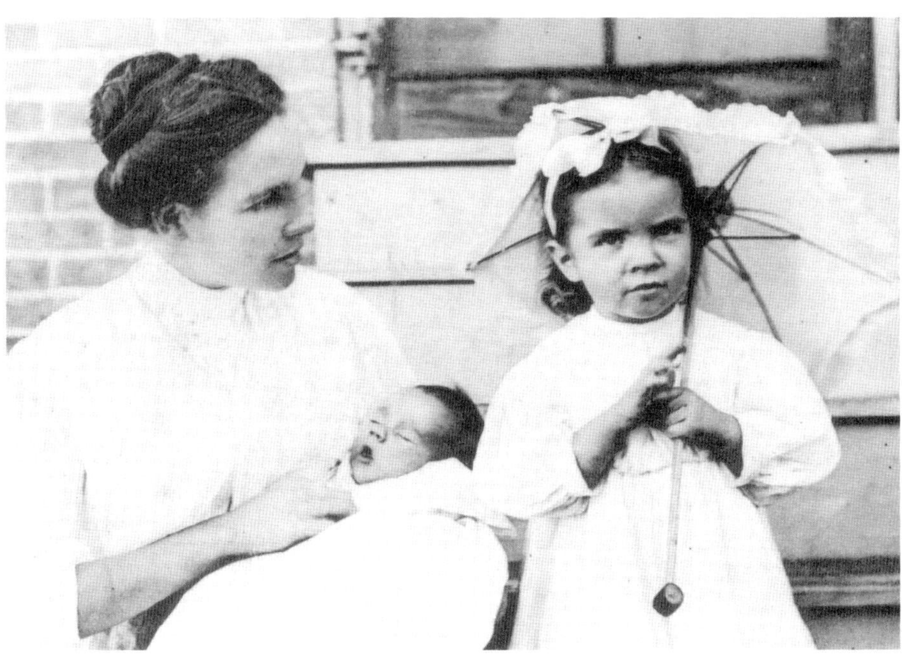

Frances Schmidt with her mother Ester just after baby Thomas was born. *Photo courtesy of Francis Schmidt Hall; provided by Jim Eckles.*

The Schmidt/McDonald ranch house prior to restoration. The window and doors are missing, the front porch and chimney collapsed and much of the stucco is missing from the outer wall. *Photo courtesy of White Sands Missile Range.*

Above: The Schmidt/ McDonald house is open to curious visitors during Trinity Test open house days. *Photo by Elva K. Österreich, 2019.*

Right: Howard McDonald's parents' house at the bombing range ranch. This is where Howard lived until the government took the land and asked the families to move in 1942. But since his father still had cattle at the location, they returned to the land until 1947 to manage the herd. *Photo courtesy Howard McDonald.*

After court battles, Dave McDonald actually returned to his home on the range in 1982, at the age of eighty-one, and tried (unsuccessfully) to take it back. "Armed with two rifles and an old pistol, an 81-year-old rancher and his niece slipped across the boundary into White Sands Missile Range at dawn Wednesday, setting up occupancy in the isolated house from which he was evicted 40 years ago," the *Albuquerque Journal* reported on October 14, 1982. The family had posted signs, stating, "Road Closed to the U.S. Army—Deeded Land, No Trespassing."

Colonel Dan Duggan was one of the missile range commanders there to deal diplomatically with the situation. He said McDonald was informed that he was unauthorized to be on government property and was given a trespass form letter. "I could tell he was about as impressed with that as if someone had squashed a mosquito," Duggan wrote for the *Hands Across History* newsletter in November 2009.

McDonald told Duggan that the army took his land in 1942 for the bombing range and later development of the atomic bomb. For years, it paid him a lease on the grassland, but in 1980, the government cut off the payments and started eminent domain hearings, condemning the land, and was ready to pay off McDonald. But he wanted something closer to $960,000 for the 640 acres than the $35,000 he was being offered by the court.

"The army never intended to give the land back. The windmill and the water well were all wrecked and requests to graze cattle were denied. They keep trying to fool people by calling it a desert while last summer the grass was knee high," McDonald told Duggan.

Ultimately, after four days of making the effort to understand McDonald and his point of view, personal visits from Congressman Joe Skeen, Senator Harrison Schmitt (also an astronaut who walked on the moon), state representative James Martin, New Mexico Cattle Growers Association president Bob Jones and Major General Fulwyler and promises of proposed legislation on behalf of the ranchers, McDonald allowed himself and his niece Mary to be escorted off the ranch and the missile range.

In the end, McDonald never got that big pot of money. Although Skeen did introduce a bill to provide the White Sands Missile Range ranchers with more money, Congress never passed it. Dave McDonald died in 1993.

Dave's brother Ross had a son, Howard McDonald, who was involved in seeking judgments in the family's favor for many years. Howard was three years old when his family was told to vacate the ranch in 1942. He doesn't remember the actual Trinity explosion, as they had moved north, near Three Rivers, by that time. Howard's family returned to the ranch for

Ross McDonald's horses at the ranch on the bombing range in the 1940s. *Photo courtesy Howard McDonald.*

Rube McDonald; George and Laura McDonald; and Carmen, Howard and Ross McDonald at the McDonald ranch on the White Sands Proving Ground bombing range (now White Sands Missile Range). The McDonald family still had cattle and went to their house on the bombing range in the years following the Trinity Test. *Photo courtesy Howard McDonald.*

Above: Howard McDonald, two years old, at the family ranch in the Oscura Mountains, August 24, 1941. *Photo courtesy Howard McDonald.*

Left: Howard McDonald on his horse in 1945 at the family ranch on the bombing range. *Photo courtesy Howard McDonald.*

Howard McDonald as a young man roping as part of the TR Branding Crew. Ranching life in the Tularosa Basin. *Photo courtesy Howard McDonald.*

A very young Howard McDonald and his grandfather Ted McDonald his Tularosa home. Ted McDonald looked out of the Tularosa home's window one day circa 1943 and, to his surprise, saw a military truck with his ranch house on the back rumbling through town toward El Paso. *Photo courtesy Howard McDonald.*

Above: Hired hand at the Mockingbird Ranch rock corral, circa 1935. *Photo courtesy of Human Systems Research and White Sands Missile Range.*

Left: An unidentified swimmer enjoying the concrete water tank at the Jose Lucero Ranch, circa 1931–36. *Photo courtesy of Human Systems Research and White Sands Missile Range.*

a time in 1943 and 1944, he said, because they had never been paid for it in the first place. His father and uncle were taken to court for refusing to stay off the ranch, but when the judge asked if they were being paid their rent for the property and the government attorneys admitted the ranchers had not been paid, the federal judge dismissed the charges and ordered the rent be paid.

Howard's dad went back to graze his cattle in 1947. Howard said, "I was just a kid; I wasn't out there, and we didn't move back out there, but my dad stayed out there."

Howard said part of the deal with the government was that the property wasn't supposed to be damaged, and nothing was supposed to be taken from the homes there. "But my grandfather's house, they did," he said. "They stole it." Howard's grandfather was Tom, father of Dave, Rube, Ross and George McDonald. Howard said his grandfather was in their Tularosa home one day and saw his own house from the range being driven toward El Paso on the back of a truck. Eventually, the family was compensated for the building, as a federal marshal was sent to find it by a judge at the Lincoln County seat of Carrizozo. An El Paso–based mover had been hired to take it south to the Fort Bliss area, where it was used as an office building.

The photos in this section, provided by Howard McDonald and others, depict ranching life in the 1940s and earlier, capturing the life left behind when war and the atomic bomb changed the world.

8

LIVING DOWNWIND

There are those in the Tularosa and Socorro areas who felt like guinea pigs in the aftermath of the Trinity explosion. This is a reference heard and seen in various accounts from those who feel there should be some recompense, or at least recognition, for the health hardships that seem to be a result of radiation and fallout in the areas involved.

"The test was the only time the government tested a bomb one hundred feet above the ground," Tularosa Basin Downwinders Consortium (TBDC) cofounder Tina Cordova said. "The reason they never did it again is because of the fallout. They believe it went seven miles past the atmosphere. It created more light than the sun, gathered up an enormous amount of plant, sand, material and took it into the air. Ash fell for days.

"They never evacuated anybody or warned anybody. From the census, there were tens of thousands of people that lived within fifty miles, and some ranchers within twelve miles. When the ash fell, it settled on everything."

Painting a picture of life in 1945, Cordova said there was no running water. People relied on cisterns for their water, used the ditch water for bathing and laundry. There were no grocery stores, only mercantiles selling basic goods like sugar, flour, rice, coffee and cereal—nothing that was refrigerated. Everything else consumed was grown or hunted.

"People went back to their lives not understanding what all this meant," she said. "They damaged us. People have been dying of cancers. We were the first people ever exposed to radiation in the world."

Tina Cordova, cofounder of the Tularosa Basin Downwinders Consortium, speaks with community members who have lost family members to cancer. The group attributes high incidences in the area to radiation from the Trinity Test. *Photo by Joan Price, 2011.*

The consortium has held annual luminaria lightings and prayer vigils to honor those affected by the blast in Tularosa and Socorro locations since its founding in 2005.

"Last year [2019] we had over 800 luminarias, and called out more than 800 names," Cordova said.

TBDC is also represented by protests each time there is a Trinity Site open house and visitors can drive in to visit the site. This happens twice a year on the first Saturdays of April and October. "We have the greatest concern for the people who were the closest to the test site and received the most exposure," Cordova said, claiming that people in Otero, Lincoln, Socorro and Sierra Counties suffer far higher rates of cancer, in some cases six to eight times the national average. "There was a time when I knew ten people in Tularosa who had brain tumors," she said. "The incidence of brain tumors in the [United States] population is one in 5,000, and Tularosa has a population of 3,500. You don't have to be a mathematician."

In 2011, Bebe Alexander (*left*) of Tularosa begins to count the number of family members in her family who died of cancer to have their names commemorated by luminarias at a candlelight vigil organized by the Tularosa Basin Downwinders Consortium. Alexander, a cancer survivor, is the only remaining member of her family and carried a candle for herself in the vigil. Rebecca Miller, writing the names down, lost her grandmother to cancer; her daughter, ten, is writing the names on the luminarias. *Photo by Joan Price.*

She said area residents who were children at the time of the detonation lived what would now be called an organic lifestyle, consuming fresh milk and locally grown food. Instead of being good for the people, the contaminated food supply made them sick. In April 2014, Cordova told a reporter, "The only story that has ever been told is the story of science and no story has ever been told about the health effects. And you know what's tragic is we have a gentleman with us, Henry Herrera, he is from Tularosa, he has been dealing with cancer for a number of years and he is in his 70s and we have this young man he is in his 20s and is in remission from leukemia. When you have long-term exposure to radiation you don't know when it is going to materialize or when it is going to strike you."

TBDC's other founder, Fred Tyler, grew up in Tularosa. He ranked fourth in his graduating class at Tularosa High School in 1968. His mother, Ruthina Utter Tyler, born and raised in Tularosa, endured three rounds of cancer

Cancer survivors and families of those who have died of cancer, possibly as a result of the Trinity Test, take part in a candlelight vigil held by the Tularosa Basin Downwinders Consortium. *Photo by Joan Price, 2011.*

of different types, finally uterine cancer. In June 2005, he wrote a letter to the *Alamogordo Daily News*, stating, "I wonder [about] the tests at Trinity Site in 1945. I wonder if the tests there had anything to do with the numerous residents of Tularosa and surrounding communities who have contracted various forms of cancer. I think someone with the resources, or some entity like the American Cancer Society, should do a study to see if there are significantly larger numbers of cancers now than before July 1945. Perhaps the DoE or the U.S. government owes compensation to all these people even though most of them were not employees at the time of the Trinity Site test."

Cordova saw the letter and contacted Tyler, and the grassroots TBDC was off and running.

"I am a cancer survivor, thyroid cancer, but I had problems before that," Cordova said. "My father, Tony Cordova, born and raised in Tularosa, developed cancer in early 2004. I have talked to my grandmothers. One of

In 2008, Tresa VanWinkle helps Fred Tyler collect cancer data for the TBDC. Tina Cordova watches behind them. VanWinkle, who has lost numerous family members to cancer, was inspired by her experience to start a grassroots nonprofit cancer prevention organization called CAPPED (Cancer Awareness, Prevalence, Prevention and Early Detection). *Photo by Joan Price.*

them told me that they were asleep [when the Trinity Test happened]. My father was getting ready for the day—the sky lit up, the whole town shook, a few days later a distinct ash settled. There are studies of wind patterns that showed wind down the Tularosa Basin as far as El Paso…and then men in funny suits came in with boxes to study."

After several phone calls between the two and others, Cordova and Tyler discussed organizing a grassroots survey to collect preliminary data on cancers not only in Tularosa but also in other communities. "If no one is willing to do it, we will have to do it ourselves. Eventually, someone will listen to us," she said.

Fifteen years later, Tyler has since passed away, but Cordova is still organizing and leading the fight. At a 2019 TBDC meeting in Tularosa, Cordova pointed out that not only did the radiation have the opportunity to affect area communities, but for a while, there was also little to keep people from visiting the site itself.

"There was a time when you could really go in and out of the Trinity Site," she said. "They took our kids out there on field trips, and they let them pack their pockets full of trinitite, and there was no concern for our health. I mean so much so that they didn't even close the site to people going out there. There is no doubt there was total lack of concern for our health."

Cordova said that in 1990, the Radiation Exposure Compensation Act was created, and $2.3 billion was paid out to downwinders of the Nevada test site, but the people of southern New Mexico "got 100 times more radiation than the Nevada test site, and we have never been included."

She said the damages have devastated the people of rural New Mexico generationally. Families affected by cancer exhaust their financial resources with medical and death issues, which prevents them from being able to pass along accumulated resources to their children.

"This is a social justice issue," she said. "We were unknowing, unwilling and uncompensated."

One of the protesters in April 2014, Lorenzo Olascoaga, twenty-two at the time, said he believes many of his own family members' cancers were due to radiation exposure from the site. "It was a chance to get the word

Tina Cordova oversees the process of gathering personal information about cancer in the area from residents during a TBDC meeting in 2012. *Photo by Joan Price.*

out," Olascoaga said. "It's not fair what they did to us. Even though we are further down the generation, it is still hard for us to carry on. We have lost a lot of family due to this. We are worried too. Nothing has happened to us now; it kind of takes a while for the effects to be seen a lot of times. It is kind of scary to think about it."

In a September 2014 story, *Alamogordo Daily News* reporter John Bear wrote about Tularosa native Henry Herrera, who was eleven years old and helping his father fill the radiator in the family truck when he heard a thunderous boom and flash of reddish fiery light on July 16, 1945. "No sooner did he close the hood on the thing, you know, and 'Kaplow,' man," Herrera said. "That was the loudest explosion I'd ever heard around this area."

Herrera told John Bear that the swirling mushroom cloud's ascent into the morning sky caught his attention and his mother's anger at having the day's wash in blowing dust. "She had her clothes hung up and here comes the damn dust," he said. "She was madder than hell. She had to wash those clothes twice."

Residents near the Trinity Site reported fallout snowing down for days afterward, covering roofs and livestock.

A previous study by the Centers for Disease Control and Prevention found that radiation exposure rates near the Trinity test were measured at ten thousand times higher than currently allowed. The dosage assessments were, however, deemed incomplete because they did not take into account internal exposure. According to the study, residents of New Mexico were not warned of the 1945 test, informed of any health hazards afterward or evacuated at any point before, during or after the test.

Herrera, eighty at the time of the interview, said it was not unusual for Tularosans to live well into their nineties, but in the years following the Trinity test, the life expectancy plummeted. Even people who weren't yet alive suffer from health problems, cancer and thyroid issues.

Herrera, who beat salivary gland cancer, believed the health problems so many residents face spring from that first nuclear test. "I can't think of anything else," he said. "It just came out of the clear blue sky."

Gloria Herrera, Henry's wife, told Bear that she was too young to remember the Trinity Test but knows that residents of Tularosa ate fresh fruit and vegetables, along with game meat like venison and rabbit because store-bought meat was too expensive. She said residents collected rainwater, dried red and green chilies on rooftops and used corn for tortillas. Staple dishes like enchiladas would have been made from homegrown chile and corn, coupled with locally produced cheese.

"Everything they consumed was mostly homegrown," she said. "This was July. You were picking apples; you were picking pears, beans."

Gloria works with TBDC because she hopes the work, vigils and protests will bring increased awareness to the world.

"It is not the treatments, it's the tears," she told another reporter. "It's the funerals, the sadness that the people in Tularosa have endured, those who have died of cancer and nobody cares. The government did this to us. The government had the bomb."

In 2015, Henry and Gloria Herrera together provided a written statement to TBDC:

> *My name is Henry Herrera, I am 81 years old. On the morning of July 16, 1945 at about 5:30 a.m. at the age of 11, I was helping my father fill the radiator of his truck with water when I witnessed the blast of what I call "the first atomic bomb."*
>
> *I heard a very large blast and saw a very big flash of light. I got so scared I thought the world is coming to an end.... Then I saw what looked like a large big black gray ball of smoke and it was huge and moving, going higher and higher in a northeasterly direction. I watched this cloud of dirt, smoke debris for many hours leaving only to get something to eat or to use the bathroom. I saw it travel to the north east toward Capitan, Ruidoso, Hondo, Roswell after a few hours it started back towards Tularosa I ran in the house to tell my mother, "Aqui viene la bola patras."* ["The ball is coming back toward Tularosa."] *My mother did not believe me, so she went outside to see for herself. My mother had already done her laundry and hung it out to dry. Because of the dirt, dust debris, black ash that fell on her clothes, she became very very angry, because she had to take all her clothes down and wash it again. This filth landed all over our town, covered our village with radiation. It was on our roofs, our gardens, milk cows, rabbits, pigs, turkeys, and chickens.*
>
> *Our water was contaminated because all we had was rainwater from the cistern and ditch water all the debris from the roof was in our cistern after the first rain fall.*
>
> *Everything we consumed was filled with radiation. At the age of 63 I became ill with cancer. I've lost my brother, a nephew, and niece to cancer. Two sisters were cancer survivors.*
>
> *Because of what I witnessed on July 16, 1945, I have been interviewed by the* Wall Street Journal, *Aljazeera TV, Chanel 7 KOAT, Japanese newspaper, two Japanese TV stations, the* Alamogordo Daily News

> *and finally 3 people from the National Cancer Institute and a doctor from UNM* [University of New Mexico] *spent 3 hours interviewing me at my home on Sept. 29, 2014.*
>
> *I'm Gloria Herrera, Henry's wife. On May 1, 1998, we found out that Henry had cancer. He was 63 years old. First came the shock, then the tears followed by prayer, oh so very many prayers....*
>
> *He had cancer of the parotid* [salivary] *gland. I have a list of 279 people from the Tularosa area that Henry and I know or knew that have had cancer, died of cancer or are cancer survivors....*
>
> *That Atomic bomb has caused anguish to so many people in New Mexico. I say we are sufferers of radiation exposure and our government should apologize to us for being abandoned to our fate. The people from New Mexico have suffered physically, mentally and financially and we are all here in hopes that you will find a way to help us.*

The following statement, provided to the TBDC, was written by Edna Kay Hinkle. It is overwhelming, but it is not unique. It is this kind of family devastation of which the downwinders are asking for acknowledgement and compensation from the United States government:

> *Richard (Dick) and Genevra Wood Gililland were White Sands Missile Range Ranchers, who were living west of Salinas Peak 27 miles from where the atomic bomb was tested. Dick died in 1962 at the age of 73 from double pneumonia. Genevra died in 1986 at the age of 94 from old age. Neither one of them ever had cancer. They had six children: Alice, Sam, Dixie, Lola, Pete and Jess. Every one of these descendants' families has been affected by cancer. Jess and Pete were asleep on the front porch when this bomb went off and woke them up. They saw the mushroom 27 miles away. The government didn't even bother to tell them to get out of the area beforehand. Jess told me the government never told them what the mushroom was.*
>
> *Sam's daughter Cleo had stomach cancer when she was 12. Alice had breast cancer when she was in her early 80s, her husband Clay died of colon cancer at the age of 66. Her daughter Lucy died from breast cancer at the age of 66. Her son Richard got prostate cancer when he was 56 and died from it when he was 73. Dixie's husband Roy died from pancreatic cancer. Her son-in-law Tony Beanblossom died from colon cancer when he was 67. Her daughter-in-law Karen Beanblossom Tucker died of breast cancer. Lola has had skin cancer. Her husband Hansel Tucker beat colon*

cancer when he was 52. Peter had cancer when he died at the age of 79. His wife Wilma was 66 when she died from pancreatic cancer.

Jess has had a skin cancer surgically removed just below his eye. I am Jess Gililland's daughter, my name is Edna Kay Hinkle. I beat breast cancer when I was 59. I have had seven skin cancers and probably hundreds of potential skins cancers cut or burnt off. My sister Judy beat breast cancer when she was 49. Now the Drs. [doctors] *tell us Mom, who also lived on the missile range, has thyroid cancer. We see the surgeon next week to have her thyroid removed. She's 83.*

My dad and mom Jess and Louise Gilliland, my dad's brother Pete Gilliland, and his wife, Wilma Gilliland walked around at the Trinity site after the bomb was detonated. They picked up the melted sand, and took it home, not knowing it was full of radiation. Back in those days they had a fence around the Trinity site, but the gate was open. Judy and I were in our mom's ovaries at the time. Judy and I both got cancer. Wilma was pregnant at the time with Shirley Ann Gilliland. Shirley was born without any eyes.

A woman lights the luminarias for a candlelight vigil held by the Tularosa Basin Downwinders Consortium, held annually at the Tularosa High School athletic field. *Photo by Joan Price, 2011.*

Alice Smith's daughter Viola told her doctor she hadn't been born yet when the bomb went off, so she doesn't have to worry about cancer. He told her the radiation altered our DNA so we are more susceptible to cancer. I heard a rumor that my oncologist came here because there is so much cancer here in the Tularosa Basin.

Genevra's brother John Wood lived on the ranch to the south of her. He died of Leukemia. His son Howard and his daughter Bonnie both died of cancer. Genevra's brother Pete Wood's ranch was to the south of John Wood's ranch. Pete's son-in-law Harvey Hinkle has liposarcoma cancer, his son Eldon Hinkle died a few months ago from esophageal cancer. Genevra's sister-in-law Annie Wood, who lived on the ranch to the north of Genevra, died of esophageal cancer. She was closer to Trinity Site than Dick's ranch.

These are just the cancer victims who are my family. The government took these ranchers land to form the White Sands Missile Range. These ranchers fought the government for years trying to get fair compensation for their ranches. They just wanted to be paid the same way the MacGregor Range Ranchers were so they could afford to go buy another ranch. Most of the White Sands Missile Range ranchers have died now....

I have two daughters. My oldest daughter, Jackie Hinkle says it's not a matter of if you get cancer; it's a matter of when.

A seven year study conducted by the National Cancer Institute, with the results published September 1, 2020 (in the journal *Health Physics*), found that despite no public notice before the test, no evacuations and a low detonation height, only small geographic areas immediately downwind of the Trinity Test received exposures of significance as judged by their magnitude relative to naturally occurring background radiation. The highest exposures would have been in Guadalupe, San Miguel, Torrance, Socorro and Lincoln Counties. All locations other than the centerline of the pattern through those counties were found to have likely received doses from Trinity at least one thousand fold lower than those in the maximum exposed locations. In addition, the study found there is no evidence to suggest transgenerational effects from Trinity.

9

RIGHT OR WRONG?

It was a terrible decision for me to make, but I made it. And I made it to save 250,000 boys for the United States, and I'd make it again under similar circumstances.
—President Harry Truman commenting on the decision to drop the Hiroshima bomb in a 1948 letter to his sister, Mary

The Szilárd petition, drafted by scientist Leo Szilárd, was signed by seventy scientists working on the Manhattan Project in Oak Ridge, Tennessee, and the Metallurgical Laboratory in Chicago, Illinois. It was circulated in July 1945 and asked President Harry S. Truman to inform Japan of the terms of surrender demanded by the Allies and allow Japan to either accept or refuse these terms before America used atomic weapons. However, the petition never made it through the chain of command to President Truman. It was not declassified and made public until 1961.

It reads, in part:

> *We, the undersigned, respectfully petition: first, that you exercise your power as Commander-in-Chief, to rule that the United States shall not resort to the use of atomic bombs in this war unless the terms which will be imposed upon Japan have been made public in detail and Japan knowing these terms has refused to surrender; second, that in such an event the question whether or not to use atomic bombs be decided by you in the light of the considerations presented in this petition as well as all the other moral responsibilities which are involved.*

Later, in 1946, Szilárd, jointly with Albert Einstein, created the Emergency Committee of Atomic Scientists, which counted among its board Linus Pauling (Nobel Peace Prize, 1962).

Born in Czechoslovakia, Lilli Hornig and her family immigrated to the United States from Berlin after her father was threatened with imprisonment in a concentration camp. She was a young chemist when her husband, Don Hornig, was personally asked by George Kistiakowsky to go to Los Alamos to work on a secret project. At first, Lilli worked on plutonium chemistry, but after concern was raised that plutonium could cause reproductive damage for women, she began working for the explosives group. A witness to the Trinity Test, she recalled the vivid colors of the blast. Lilli is one of the seventy who signed the petition to have a demonstration of the bomb's destruction rather than dropping it on Japan.

> *During the Trinity test—I knew it was coming up and in fact, two days before they'd had a malfunction down there, an early misfire on the X unit. And at two o'clock in the morning our group leader, Lewis Fussell, was knocking on my bedroom window saying, "You have to get up, we have some work to do."*
>
> *But anyway, I had planned to drive up to Sandia Mountain, which had a nice road to the top and a clear view 110 miles down to the Trinity site. Some friends came with me…Betty Thomas…and David Anderson who was also part of the X group. And so the three of us—our car couldn't have taken more than three—were up there, and we knew it was—the shot was scheduled to go off before sunrise in order to—for all the cameras to function properly.*
>
> *And so there we sat at ten thousand feet and we slept a little, we put sleeping bags on the ground. None of us slept very well and so we got up about three o'clock, I guess, and started waiting for the shot, keeping our eyes glued on the site. And we waited and waited and at 4:30 the sun rose. And we were so crushed and disappointed and said, "Well, I guess it's not going to go today," and we had to go back up through the hill and get to work. And so, we packed up our sleeping bags and got in the car. It didn't take long, I mean, it was quick decision, and I was sitting in the car reaching for my ignition key—and the thing bloomed in front of us. And of course, we had neglected the fact that at ten thousand feet the sun rises earlier than it does at two thousand or three thousand down in the desert. So, we blamed ourselves for not being good scientists there, but we did see it and it was just incredible.*

> *Just a couple of nights ago I saw a film on PBS of the superbomb tests and it reminded me very strongly, and of course the scale is far bigger, but the pictures are much like what I remember in my mind as the—these sort of boiling clouds and color—vivid colors like violet, purple, orange, yellow, red, just everything. It was fantastic. And we were all kind of shaken up but—and we waited for the shock wave to come, which it did, requisite, I don't know—eleven, twelve, fifteen minutes later.*
>
> *But when the bomb was dropped we were—Don and I were actually in Milwaukee visiting his family because his brother was in the Navy and was slated to be shipped out and this was his leave, just a few days before showing up at the West coast. And we knew damn well he wasn't going to be going anywhere, much at least not into danger, and we knew that the drop was imminent. We didn't know the precise moment. Certainly Don's parents didn't have TV at the time and I don't know if there were ever any news on, but Don and I went downtown. There were all the papers with the headlines, so we knew it had gone off.*
>
> *That was an odd mix of feelings. I mean, certainly some triumph and the destruction was just so incredible. I think we've all been a little haunted by that over the years.*

Herbert Lehr (1922–2018) was a special engineer in the physics division and helped set up the McDonald ranch house for the Trinity Test and then helped transport and assemble the Gadget's plutonium core at the site. When he returned to the site in 2005 for its sixtieth anniversary, he talked about his experience to the Associated Press.

> *All of a sudden this very bright light came out and where I was, it was intense enough that the whole mountain range itself was completely whited out. I took the smoke glass and turned around and looked at it, and I could see the ball and fire rising up It was sort of awe inspiring.*
>
> *In a lot of respects I felt as if I had done something worthwhile. I am in no way ashamed of what I had done in any way, shape, matter or form. I did what I was told to do. I did it to the best of my ability.*

In a July 17, 1983 *El Paso Time*s story, Pat Henry asked printer Jack Coulehan about his thoughts on the dropping of the bomb on Japan.

Coulehan said he realized that he witnessed the dawning of the nuclear age after the bombs were dropped on August 6 in Hiroshima and August 9 in Nagasaki, Japan. "At the time, the decision to use the weapon was absolutely

Despite being rebuilt, the Schmidt/McDonald Ranch house retains much of the sense of what it must have been like in 1945. Work benches and table were installed at the time. To keep dust and sand out of instruments and tools, the windows were covered with plastic and tape was used to fasten the edges of the plastic and to seal doors and cracks in the walls. *Photo by Elva K. Österreich, 2019.*

correct," he said. "We had relatives in the war. When Truman pulled the plug, it ended the war. But now it looks like it's got away from us. Frankly, I have no answers."

On July 12, 1970, Associated Press science writer Bill Stockton wrote about the twenty-five years since the Trinity explosion: "Four weeks later [following the Trinity test] two Japanese cities lay in rubble and World War II had ended. World politics would never be the same again. The alumni of Trinity are scattered now, but their legacy lives on. It glides beneath the oceans in a submarine powered by a silent reactor and carrying nuclear-tipped missiles. It beats in the breast of a woman in France, whose life depends on a tiny atomic generator regulating her heartbeat. It beacons a power-hungry world as the only salvation when conventional energy sources are dead. And it is inexorably entwined in a complex struggle to preserve earth's environment for generations hence."

Stockton spoke to some of those who were present at the explosion about their feelings on the aftermath.

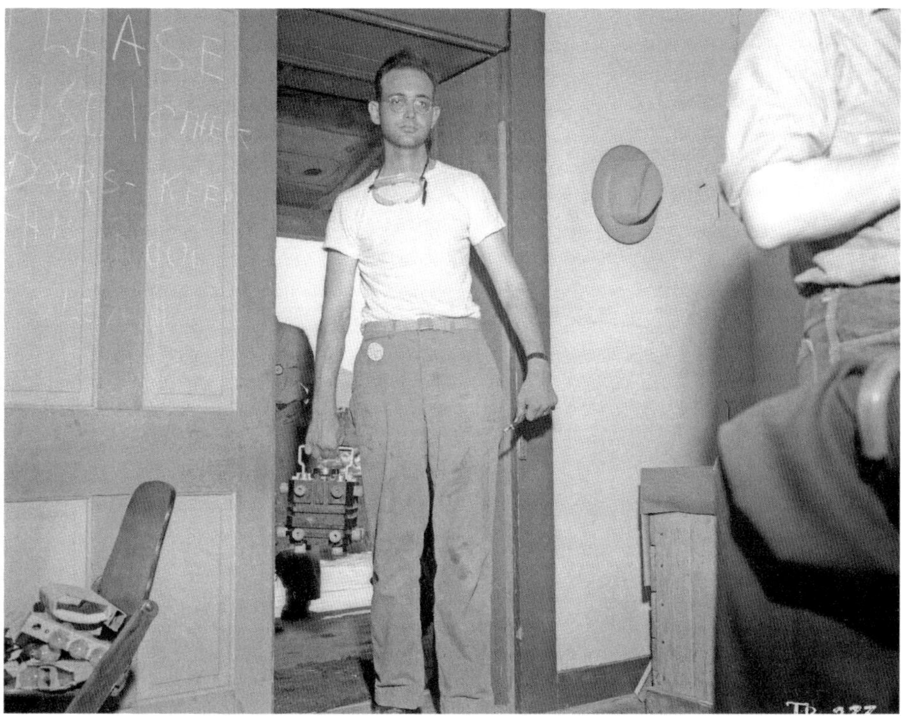

Herb Lehr takes plutonium hemispheres into the assembly room at the Schmidt/McDonald ranch house. The chalked message on the door reads "Please use other doors—keep this room clean." *Photo courtesy of Los Alamos National Laboratories.*

Vannevar Bush, born in 1890, was at Trinity base camp, ten miles southwest of the tower, lying on a canvas spread over the wet ground. An electrical engineer from the Massachusetts Institute of Technology, Bush was head of the Office of Scientific Research and Development. He oversaw an army of thirty thousand working on radar, the proximity fuse and a flock of defense projects including the $2 billion Manhattan Project. "Our fear was that Hitler would get it first," Bush said. "If Hitler had gotten the bomb into production before we did, he would have conquered the world. I think it's a damn good thing we have the bomb and the Russians have it. Because now, no ruling group will commit suicide, knowing they're doing so."

Norris Bradbury was responsible for assembly of the gadget after battling sand and stifling heat, readying the device in the final, frustrating week. "They moved all of us who had nothing to do with the control point off about 10 miles to a hillside. It was drizzling and we kind of huddled in the sleeping bags and I went to sleep. Thank goodness someone woke me up.

The icehouse attached to the Schmidt/McDonald house, where the plutonium core was assembled prior to the Trinity Test. *Photo by Elva K. Österreich, 2019.*

J. Robert Oppenheimer receives the 1963 Enrico Fermi Award from President Lyndon B. Johnson at a White House ceremony on December 2, 1963. *Photo courtesy of the U.S. Department of Energy.*

The thing that impressed me particularly, that was the brightness of the light. It was beyond belief in terms of any other thing I'd seen," he recalled.

Bradbury later succeeded Oppenheimer at Los Alamos when Oppenheimer resigned after the war. "One of the most significant things done after Trinity was development of the hydrogen bomb," Bradbury said. "You might think, 'Oh, my God that's terrible.' But nevertheless, if we hadn't done it, somebody else would have. We would have been on the receiving end of that sort of system rather than where we are."

Los Alamos pioneer Jim Tuck, born sixty years earlier, while not directly involved in the test, rode with three old army busses from Los Alamos to the desert. They waited through the night on a hill twenty miles from Ground Zero. After the test, the return bus ride was solemn. "We realized what we had done," Tuck said. "And we wondered what would have happened to the world if we hadn't done it and someone else had."

Frank DiLuzzio was ordered to Los Alamos in 1944 by the army engineers. "I didn't know what A-bomb meant," he said. "I thought it was a code or something. But when that damn thing went off, I knew it wasn't just another weapon. I thought, 'My God, we've ignited the atmosphere.' If I hadn't been a religious man, I know I'd have been thinking about religion. It makes you feel about the size of an ant."

Stanislaw Ulam decided not to go on the bus and stayed in Los Alamos. "Somehow, I didn't feel like going," he said. "It was purely nervous or psychological. A sort of block if you want to call it that."

He remembered the buses' return. "You could tell at once they had had a strange experience. You could see it on their faces," he said. "I saw that something very grave and strong had happened to [affect their] whole outlook on the future. There are two great mysteries in the universe. One is astronomy, the science of the skies, two more ways to explore the universe external to us. The other is the study of the nuclei of the atom, the physics of matter. The study of the nucleus is really a study of the universe, all these new particles about which one knows so little. These are called fundamental particles, but probably we will discover they are not so fundamental."

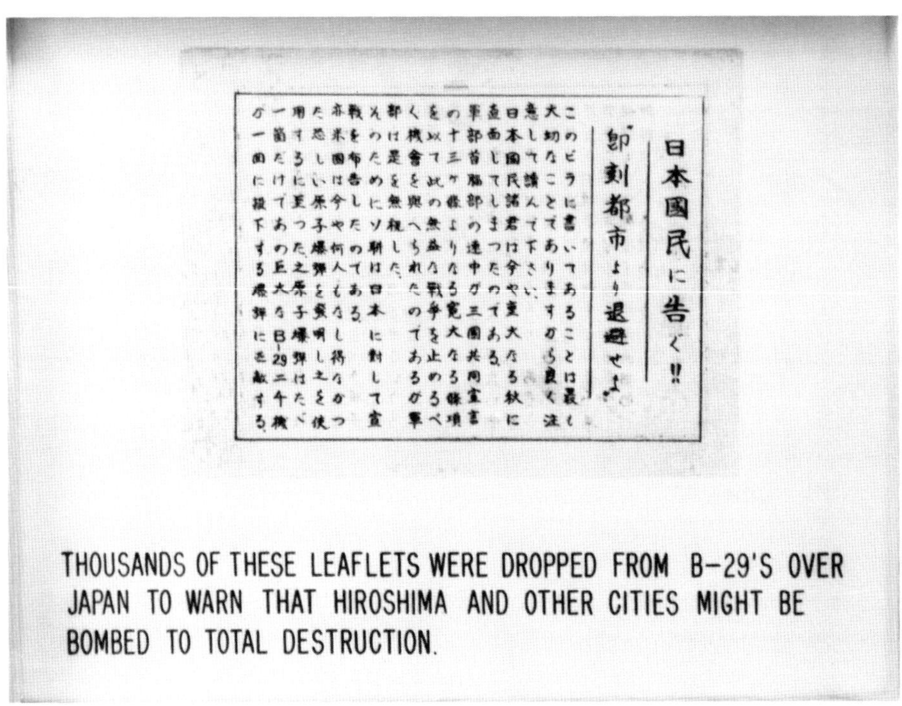

An example of leaflets that were dropped on Japan prior to the bombing of Hiroshima and Nagasaki. *Photo courtesy of New Mexico State University Library, Archives and Special Collections.*

On Sunday, August 5, 1984, the *El Paso Times* printed a story about Charles Sweeney, who piloted the bomber that dropped the deadly load over Nagasaki. The story, titled "Nagasaki Pilot Hopes He Wrote Final Chapter," reflects the views of many on the bombing of Japan. The story, out of the Associated Press, had a Boston dateline.

"I'd like to see none of this used again," Sweeney said. The former army air corps pilot saw "the awful spectacle of brilliantly colored mushroom clouds racing across the skies."

On August 6, 1945, Sweeney watched while the first atomic bomb was dropped on Hiroshima, killing about seventy-five thousand people. Thousands of others subsequently died from radiation poisoning and other effects. Three days later, the twenty-five-year-old captain piloted his B-29 Superfortress, The Great Artiste, over the hilly coastal city of Nagasaki and gave the final command to drop the second atomic bomb on Japan.

"In 52 seconds, the city had vanished under a nuclear cloud. Some 78,000 people are believed to have been killed or injured in the blast," the story said. "Sweeney has no regrets. The planned invasion of Japan—with estimates of a million casualties—was three months away. The bomb was seen as a way of saving U.S. and Japanese lives."

"I've had Japanese people thank me for what I did," Sweeney said. "They wanted the war to end, but their leaders wanted to continue the fighting. The bomb changed all that."

Sweeney was on the Pacific island of Tinian when word came that the first mission was set for August 6 over Hiroshima. He was to pilot a bomber over the target and release three instrument canisters that would measure the effects of the blast. When he dropped the canisters, Sweeney had only fifty-two seconds to get out of the way before the bomb fell to 1,500 feet and detonated.

"It seemed like more time had passed and I began to wonder if it was going to work. Then we saw the tremendous flash," he recalled. Those in the planes saw the sky turn a bright blue white, and the planes were rocked by rings of hot vapor rushing from the blast. The planes circled back over the target to see the effect of the bomb.

"Off to the right, there were a big bunch of crummy-looking black clouds," Sweeney said. "Above them was a vertical cloud with every color in the rainbow—red, blue, yellow and green—seething and billowing up to 25,000 feet. It was very awesome, a fantastic awesome sight. There was a sense of elation, a sense that maybe this would shorten the war."

Three days later, Sweeney was over Japan again, this time with Fat Boy in his plane's bomb bay, destined for Nagasaki.

Left: Japanese Buddhist monks visited Ground Zero at Trinity Site on the sixtieth anniversary of the atomic bombing of Nagasaki in 2005. The burning of a sacred cloth scroll signified the unification of the Trinity Site and Hiroshima and Nagasaki. The flame was then extinguished, symbolically bringing the unleashing of nuclear power full circle. The original flame was lit from flames from the atomic bombing of Hiroshima sixty years before. *Photo by Ellis Neel.*

Below: The Reverend Daijho Ota leads a group of Japanese Buddhist monks as they arrive at Trinity Site on August 6, 2005. Ota, dressed in black robes and walking solemnly, carried a red and black dictionary-sized box. *Photo by Ellis Neel.*

Following the symbolic burning of a sacred cloth scroll at the location of the Trinity Site on August 6, 2005, the Reverend Daijho Ota opened the red-and-black box, here presented at the site's memorial obelisk. The box had four compartments. The monks put the ashes from the scroll and dirt from the site into it. Three sections of the ashes were sent to Hiroshima, Nagasaki and a museum in the United States. The remaining ashes were divided into eight parts and sent to the heads of countries that possess nuclear capabilities. *Photo by Ellis Neel.*

According to John Hersey in his book *Hiroshima*, which came out in 1946:

> *A surprising number of the people of Hiroshima remained more or less indifferent about the ethics of using the bomb. Possibly they were too terrified by it to want to think about it at all. Not many of them even bothered to find out much about what it was like. Mrs. Nakamura's conception of it—and awe of it—was typical. "The atom bomb," she would say when asked about it, "is the size of a matchbox. The heat of it was six thousand times that of the sun. It exploded in the air. There is some radium in it. I don't know just how it works, but when the radium is put together, it explodes." As for the use of the bomb, she would say, "It was war and we had to expect*

it." And then she would add, "Shikata ga nai," a Japanese expression as common as, and corresponding to, the Russian word "nichevo": "It can't be helped. Oh, well. Too bad." Dr. Fujii said approximately the same thing about the use of the bomb to Father Kleinsorge one evening, in German: "Da ist nichts zu machen. There's nothing to be done about it."

Many citizens of Hiroshima, however, continued to feel a hatred for Americans which nothing could possibly erase. "I see," Dr. Sasaki once said, "that they are holding a trial for war criminals in Tokyo just now. I think they ought to try the men who decided to use the bomb and they should hang them all."

Father Kleinsorge and the other German Jesuit priests, who, as foreigners, could be expected to take a relatively detached view, often discussed the ethics of using the bomb. One of them, Father Siemes, who was out at Nagatsuka at the time of the attack, wrote in a report to the Holy See in Rome, "Some of us consider the bomb in the same category as poison gas and were against its use on a civilian population. Others were of the opinion that in total war, as carried on in Japan, there was no difference between civilians and soldiers, and that the bomb itself was an effective force tending to end the bloodshed, warning Japan to surrender and thus to avoid total destruction. It seems logical that he who supports total war in principle cannot complain of a war against civilians. The crux of the matter is whether total war

The National Museum of Nuclear Science & History in Albuquerque, New Mexico, houses a look at some of the lasting effects of the atomic blast in Hiroshima and Nagasaki, like this license plate heavily damaged by the blast. *Photo by Elva K. Österreich, 2019.*

in its present form is justifiable, even when it serves a just purpose. Does it not have material and spiritual evil as its consequences which far exceed whatever good might result? When will our moralists give us a clear answer to this question?"

They died in silence, with no grudge, setting their teeth to bear it. All for the Country!

—Mr. Kiyoshi Tanimoto

BIBLIOGRAPHY

Bird, Kai, and Martin J. Sherwin. *American Prometheus: The Triumph and Tragedy of J. Robert Oppenheimer*. New York: Vintage Books, 2006.

Court, Darren, and the White Sands Missile Range Museum. *White Sands Missile Range*. Charleston, SC: Arcadia Publishing, 2009.

Eckles, Jim. *Trinity: The History of an Atomic Bomb National Historic Landmark*. Las Cruces, NM: Fiddlebike Partnership, 2015.

Eidenbach, Peter L., and Beth Morgan. *Homes on the Range: Oral Recollections of Early Ranch Life on the U.S. Army White Sands Missile Range, New Mexico*. Tularosa, NM: Human Systems Research, 1997.

Eidenbach, Peter L., and Linda Hart. *School Days: Education During the Ranching Era on the U.S. Army White Sands Missile Range, New Mexico*. Tularosa, NM: Human Systems Research, 1997.

Frisch, Otto. *What Little I Remember*. Cambridge, UK: Cambridge University Press, 1979.

Goodchild, Peter. J. *Robert Oppenheimer Shatterer of Worlds*. Boston: Houghton Mifflin, 1981.

Groves, Leslie. *Now It Can Be Told: The Story of the Manhattan Project*. New York: Da Capo Press, 1983.

Hales, Peter Bacon. *Atomic Spaces Living on the Manhattan Project*. Urbana, IL: University of Chicago Press, 1997.

Hamm, Ron. *The Bursums of New Mexico Four Generations of Leadership and Service*. Socorro, NM: Manzaneres Street Publishing, 2012.

Heitzler, Gretchen. *Meanwhile Back at the Ranch*. Albuquerque, NM: Hidden Valley Press,1980.

Hersey, John. *Hiroshima*. New York: Alfred A. Knopf, 1946.

Kelly, Cynthia C., ed. *The Manhattan Project: The Birth of the Atomic Bomb in the Words of Its Creators, Eyewitnesses, and Historians*. New York: Black Dog & Leventhal Publishers, 2007.

Kunetka, James. *City of Fire: Los Alamos and the Birth of the Atomic Age, 1943–1945*. Albuquerque: University of New Mexico Press, 1978

———. *The General and the Genius: Groves and Oppenheimer, the Unlikely Partnership that Built the Atom Bomb*. Washington, D.C.: Regenery Publishing, 2015.

Lamont, Lansing. *The Day of Trinity*. New York: Athenium, 1965.

Lapp, Ralph E. *My Life with Radiation: Hiroshima Plus Fifty Years*. Madison, WI: Cogito, 1995.

Laurence, William L. *Dawn over Zero: The Story of the Atomic Bomb*. New York: Alfred A. Knopf, 1947.

Los Alamos National Laboratory. *Los Alamos: Beginning of an Era, 1943–1945*. Los Alamos, NM: Scientific Lab, 1979.

Melnick, A.G. *They Changed the World: People of the Manhattan Project*. Foreword by Governor Bill Richardson. Albuquerque, NM: Sunstone Press, 2006.

Merlan, Thomas. *The Trinity Experiments*. Tularosa, NM: Human Systems Research, 1997.

Szasz, Ferenc Morton. *The Day the Sun Rose Twice: The Story of the Trinity Site Nuclear Explosion, July 16, 1945*. Albuquerque: University of New Mexico Press, 1984.

Townsend, David. *You Take the Sundials and Give Me the Sun*. Alamogordo, NM: Alamogordo Daily News, 1984.

Wilson, Jane, and Charlotte Serber. *Standing by and Making Do, Women of Wartime Los Alamos*. Los Alamos, NM: Los Alamos Historical Society, 1988.

INDEX

ABOUT THE AUTHOR

Elva K. Österreich is a journalist, photographer and editor in southern New Mexico. She has written hundreds of articles about the state's history, people and environment, and she especially loves the stories she hears from the old-timers. Österreich is a board member of the New Mexico Humanities Council, vice president of the Native Plant Society Otero chapter, has a poetry blog (elvasworld.blogspot.com) and has served as a La Leche League leader and as an organizer with the Alamogordo Speaker's Series.